FEAR AND LOATHING ON THE OCHE

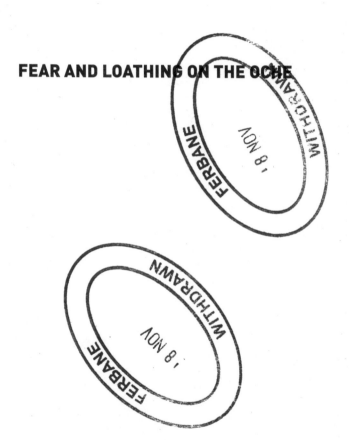

FEAR AND LOATHING ON THE OCHE

A Gonzo Journey Through the World of Championship Darts

KING ADZ

YELLOW JERSEY PRESS
LONDON

1 3 5 7 9 10 8 6 4 2

Yellow Jersey Press, an imprint of Vintage
20 Vauxhall Bridge Road
London SW1V 2SA

Yellow Jersey Press is part of the Penguin Random House group of companies
whose addresses can be found at global.penguinrandomhouse.com.

Copyright © King ADZ 2017

First published by Yellow Jersey Press in 2017

www.vintage-books.co.uk

A CIP catalogue record for this book is available from the British Library

ISBN 9781787290013

Typeset in India by Integra Software Services Pvt. Ltd, Pondicherry

Printed and bound by Clays Ltd, St Ives PLC

Penguin Random House is committed to a sustainable future
for our business, our readers and our planet. This book is
made from Forest Stewardship Council® certified paper.

For Beardie,
who will always be my champion.

CONTENTS

PROLOGUE

It's been almost two weeks of solid darts and drinking and dabbing and more darts and then a party or two where most people are talking about the darts and right here right now I am high as a kite stood slap bang in the middle of the arena in Alexandra Palace surrounded by a few thousand people – most of whom are dressed in some very professional, mind-bending costumes but all of whom are about to lose their shit. The Simpsons are in the row to my left but for some reason Bart has outgrown Homer and it's Lisa who – a little out of character – has just steamed back in after smoking back-to-back Mayfairs, ensuring she doesn't get caught short when the action begins for real. Marge has pulled off her mask as she's feeling a little the worse for wear but after she takes a couple of deep breaths her nausea seems to pass. Woody from *Toy Story* makes a dash for the toilets, almost wiping out a platoon of Stormtroopers who are speed-marching back to their seats in tight formation after completing a heroic mission to the bar for an imperial amount of lager and sufficient depth charges to take out the *Death Star*. The music is slowly and subtly getting louder, faster, stronger. The classic pop-house banger of The Chemical Brothers' 'Galvanize' increases the pace before seamlessly blending into an almost inevitable house remix of Gala's 'Free from Desire', which gees-up the gang of Little Alexes from *Clockwork Orange* – each one complete with cod piece, bowler hat, singular eyelashes and nobbling stick (how did they get them through security?).

Back to the music building and building and building and just after it cuts back to a snatch of the housey-chanty chorus of 'da da da da da da' I take a quick sip of my shandy and wipe my brow. By now I'm sweating like the proverbial pig under my heavy costume. The atmosphere is what you'd call electric, with a buzz of anticipation zapping around the place, generated, no doubt, by all the static bright plastic being worn, not to mention the music, the lager, the tension. And just after the anthemic sing-a-long lines of 'Chase the Sun' by Planet Funk drops once more, the lights go out ...

... the hall the size of an aircraft hangar goes pitch black ...

... and just for a moment ...

... all is quiet ...

CHAPTER ONE

DARTS, INNIT?

'You can take the darts out of the pub, but you can never take the pub out of the darts.'

Martin Adams, Bobby George,
Dr Patrick Chapin, et al.

'Darts is something that they can never tame,' I tell some actor in a pub just off Tottenham Court Road after he asks what I'm up to and I mention this book. 'It's the only sport they can never really clean up and remove the smell of the pub.' By the time I've finished spouting this line he might just be changing his mind about darts, and makes a face like De Niro, as if to say, Blimey – perhaps there is something interesting in there after all.

One night, hundreds of years ago, in an inn or tavern that wouldn't look out of place in the 'hood of Robin, a soldier who'd supped one too many meads (or whatever the tipple of choice was back then) snapped a few arrows he'd nicked from his mate's quiver and lobbed them towards the bottom of an empty barrel that someone had kicked on its side. One of the darts went reasonably near the centre 'eye' but the others fell on the floor. His mate clocked this attempt through the fog of alcohol and tobacco smoke and immediately spotted a challenge (because that's what soldiers do). 'I can do better than that.' And after reclaiming the broken arrows, he threw them – one by one – at the target, almost hitting the 'eye' twice. That night something took hold of those weary drunken warriors as they played their newly discovered game over and over, until the landlord lost his patience and turfed them out into the cold English night, broken arrows and all.

By contrast, the modern world of darts is a £50-million industry – the majority of this revenue coming from sponsorship, live events and television rights. It also generates tens of millions of pounds as an export, as the sport is rapidly gaining popularity across the world in countries as far-reaching as Thailand, China, India, Zimbabwe and South Africa. Even the USA can't ignore the potential revenue up for grabs if darts can somehow tip into the mainstream across the pond. The fortunes of darts – as we know it today – have been anything but steady, yet since the early twentieth century, when breweries began organising darts leagues, one relationship has remained: as mentioned above, darts and boozers go hand in hand.

It wasn't always like this. After our year-dot moment in that crusty old ale house, this exotic new pastime took several centuries to ripple out across the land, but by the 1800s a primitive game of 'darts' was being played across England and France (both countries were ruled by much the same dynasty back then) under a number of different permutations. At this stage, there was no uniformity to the rules except that the board was round and you threw some kind of stubby arrow at it. At some point towards the beginning of the nineteenth century, travelling French fairgrounds adopted it as a game of skill – you had to score under 21 points to win a prize. Being a carny game, this was naturally much harder than it looked, especially since missing the relatively small scoring part of the board resulted in an extra 18 points being added to your tally. The arrangement of the numbers on the board, on first glance, appeared random, but it was actually designed to penalise the player for their inaccuracy. The darts were called 'flechettes', which means small arrow, and by the middle of the nineteenth century the game had crossed the channel and become an integral part of the typical British fairground. The French began to manufacture darts in around 1860 and as the game rose in popularity, they began to export them from Northern France to Britain, where more and more people were beginning to play. You'd be right to speculate that they were perhaps practising at home so they could win at the fair …

There are two theories about what happened next. The first theory is that in 1896 a carpenter from Bury called Brian Gamlin (now there's a darts name if ever there was one) designed a numbered board that is still in use today. It was created following the basic premise that the high numbers were placed next to the low ones so the player paid the price for inaccuracy. The top score was the bullseye. In essence, Gamlin took the original French board, added a bullseye and called it his own.

Theory Two is that in 1913, Thomas William Buckle (again a fine name that lends itself to our beloved sport. Today he'd be called 'The Buckle', renowned for putting a tight squeeze on his opponents), a domino maker from Yorkshire, created what is now called the 'Yorkshire board'. This was identical to today's board but without the doubles and trebles. So again, remarkably similar to Gamlin's, which as we've already established was based on the original French design. To quote the Beastie Boys – 'what comes around goes around'.

The next stage in the evolution of darts followed swiftly in 1898 when Nathan P. McKenney, of Dixon, in the County of Lee, Illinois, USA, created a paper-folded dart flight.

'My invention relates to toys and games, and particularly to a game apparatus of the "dart and target" type, and has for its object to provide a dart, adapted to be projected manually, whereof the feather is of four-wing construction and is formed from a foldable blank of paper or other flexible material to adapt it to be replaced with facility,' McKenney wrote on his patent application form. This was quickly followed by a patented metal dart barrel in the UK. From that point on, there was no looking back. The board we know and love today is there for all to admire, and the dart flies through the air towards it with a lot more accuracy, even if there is some haziness about the true origins. It's probably French, let's leave it at that.

You'll be pleased to know this is where the ancient history lesson ends.

To the uninitiated, the actual physical activity of darts, its metronomic repetitiveness, could frankly make spectating the game somewhat dull. Pull away from the board a bit and the view doesn't get much better: two people throwing some rolled brass, steel or tungsten at a cork circle stuck to the wall at a certain height from a very specific distance. Swing the camera 180 degrees and you will see a somewhat younger crowd drinking, shouting, tooting, singing – some dressed as popular cartoon or promotional characters, some just giving it large in their finest designer clothes. It's 100 per cent working class and 100 per cent popular culture – a bona fide cultural movement to be recognised and documented as any other. The crowd is 90 per cent white and 70 per cent male. Why is it so white? And why, when the actual sport is so repetitive, is it so popular?

One thing is undisputed: the popularity of darts is yet again on the rise, as the sport seems to keep dipping in and out of the mainstream – the last peak was in the late seventies/early eighties. What's more, there's no doubt that it's coming back in a bigger and louder and way more raucous manner. A question that keeps nagging me – and nagging those who participate at both the professional and the amateur level – is whether darts is destined to remain forever on the fringes of contemporary sport. Will it ever really be accepted as a 'proper' sport?

The game is unquestionably wrapped around the extraordinary personas that the players adopt – what they represent, how they behave when they win or lose and, probably most importantly, how they react under pressure – even though we all know that these outlandish characters are as manufactured as the oversized and lairy shirts they play in.

There is no denying that the heritage of darts is rooted in the (now declining) pub culture of Britain. When you look at the names, the characters, the epic battles, the feuds, the classic rags-to-riches storylines where working-class men can actually 'make something' of themselves, a slightly more complex, more intriguing narrative comes into view. The five-time World Champion Eric Bristow taking an unemployed Phil Taylor under his wing and mentoring him to become the greatest ever champion mirrors the story of a prodigal son. Alan Evans emerging from the Rhondda Valley and rising to become the first superstar of darts undoubtedly has echoes of David and Goliath.

In this world, the venues – the landscapes for these epic battles – are rarely exotic, but they are real, they are industrial and they are predominantly northern; well grody, in other words. In its way, though, to the insider, this is a grand landscape. The landmark clubs etched deep into the desk of darts history speak for themselves:

Heart of the Midlands, Nottingham – now the legendary Rock City

Jollees Cabaret Club, Stoke-on-Trent – a Wilkinson's department store today

Blackpool Winter Gardens – the stag-and-hen-do Vegas of the north

The Circus Tavern – once the jewel in the Essex crown, now a lap-dancing club

Lakeside Country Club – controversially known as 'Lakeshite' by some

Alexandra Palace – uncontroversially claimed as the pinnacle of darts by others

Three in the north, three down south. All places I will visit, revisit and get to know a lot better by the time I'm done.

*

Darts in Britain was always at home in the pub, and at the start of the twentieth century the pub was the centre of the community. You could always find a variety of games to play in the boozer; it was what you did. You drank and you played. No television. Cinema was still a twinkle in the eyes of the Lumière Brothers, the variety halls offered live entertainment – singing and dancing, magic and acrobats – but the heart of the conversation was found down your local. Naturally, as darts became more and more popular it found a home in every pub.

In 1924 the National Darts Association was formed in London. It standardised the sport, laid out the rules and regulations, and helped many pubs form their own teams. For all the purists out there, the first organised and regulated competitive darts tournament was played in England when the 'Darts Challenge Cup', sponsored by *News of the World* and CN Kidd & Sons brewery, was held in London, and won by William Jewiss who hailed from Dagenham.

By 1938 the event attracted over 280,000 entrants, with over 14,500 spectators cramming into the Royal Agricultural Hall in Islington to watch, but then the Second World War put a temporary halt to all competition. When it re-started in 1947 as the News of the World Individual Darts Championship – the championship every darts player wanted to win – it was held at Alexandra Palace. The winner that year was a Harry Leadbetter of St Helens, who no doubt pocketed about three quid and spent it before he'd got to the bottom of the hill on which Ally Pally is built.

By the mid 1950s there were well over 600,000 applicants each year, which throws up the question: how did they deal with those logistics without the use of computers? The answer to this is that the *News of the World* employed a team of women to keep the applicants in some kind of order, to run the mailing list, and to keep the players in the loop via the postal system.

Popular tastes were changing, and this is something that plays a big part in the story of darts. The fact that a tabloid was its first-ever sponsor positions the game firmly in the mainstream, and even though there is some archive film of the Queen Mother throwing a few arrows to show she was at one with her people, before the 1970s, darts was rarely embraced outside of its natural home – a working-class pub – no matter how popular it got.

In April 1972, Alexandra Palace was the venue for darts' first appearance on national TV – London Weekend Television's *World of Sport* – and this momentous event propelled the sport into another dimension. Behold 12,000 fans in the building (most of whom looked like the Bay City Rollers, with their vibrantly patterned shirts dangling open, huge flares, and some very scary stack heels, all supping those minuscule cans of Ind Coope Double Diamond pale ale) and a record-breaking seven million watching on the box at home. It was after this historic televised moment that the whole concept of big-money sponsorship of the sport began to take shape in the mind of brand managers. The word was spreading and the first darts superstars were created.

'Twelve thousand darts fans turn up at the Ally Pally as drunk as skunks. They cheer on their heroes just like a football crowd. They have banners, gonks, rattles, the lot. It will be great telly.' That's how legendary television producer Donald Baverstock sold it.

It was around this time (1973) that the British Darts Organisation (BDO) was formed by Olly Croft. As he put it: 'Everybody wanted to play darts. It was very addictive and if you get involved you become very passionate. We tried to encourage women and kids to come and everything. We made it a big family thing, and that was the start of what we call the BDO family.'

'Olly Croft shook my hand and smiled,' Sid Waddell, one of the most iconic commentators, recalled in his autobiography, *Bellies and Bullseyes*. 'I was not sure what to make of him. He spoke with a rough cockney twang and was reckoned to be the owner of a profitable tile company. He told anybody who would listen that he wanted to be the "Alf Ramsey of Darts". His dictatorial attitude to the players when he did become darts supremo was to be at the heart of the dispute that ripped darts apart twenty years later.'

The role of the BDO was to gather together sixty-nine different regional/county darts organisations in order to make sure they all behaved in a unified manner, adhering to strict rules and following a rigid code of conduct, which was vital for the sport to grow and, more importantly, move swiftly and seamlessly from the fringes and into the commercial mainstream. No rogues, no spivs, no wild cards, and definitely no unregulated gambling. Croft wanted it all in-house and tightly controlled. He had spotted a gap in the market into which darts would fit nicely and he wanted to own it lock, stock and rolled brass-barrel.

'My introduction to the BDO was playing Leighton Rees at Mardy Workmen's Hall for as much as four thousand pounds. Not our money. The punters' money. They would make two queues and put money on who they thought would win. That's how it all started,' John 'Old Stoneface' Lowe, ten times World Champion, recalls.

The above quote may make it sound like some dodgy back-room deal run by illegal bookies, but it was actually a BDO-sanctioned event, and took place during the most rigorously controlled period of darts.

'Without Olly Croft, darts would not be where it is today,' Dr Patrick Chaplin, darts historian, said in the film *Blood on the Carpet*. 'The sponsors just queued up. The people couldn't get enough of darts, the sponsors couldn't get enough of darts, TV companies couldn't get enough of darts.' Which shows how, in a very short space of time, darts had become big business and was ready to be exploited.

Television played a major role in the commercialisation of the game, and one of the main factors behind this was that tournaments were cheap to produce. Matches were broadcast as a split screen with one camera on the player and another on the board, and even when a third camera was added to focus on the crowd, the production costs were never going to break the bank. Croft also realised that the audience and scope of darts could be enlarged by millions by simply televising the big events, and when this began to happen, he hoped that the BDO would become a household name, along with the top players.

Olly Croft was the mutton-chopped captain of the good ship darts and ruled it for twenty years with a rod of iron, and although most credit him with taking darts into the national arena, some say that he was only doing this for his own gain and – as we shall see – he became so besotted by his role that when he eventually and inevitably lost touch, he refused to relinquish power and go quietly.

Barry Hearn tells it like it is: 'We call them the blazers. They are in love with their sport, without a doubt, but they have no commercial expertise whatsoever, and they will never listen to anyone who has because it detracts from their own importance. Olly Croft ran the BDO as his own fiefdom. They've all got this snob value and it comes from him. When I took over the PDC (Professional Darts Corporation) in 2003 the first thing I did was send an email to Olly saying, "I appreciate there has been a lot of bad feeling on both sides, which I was never part of. Can I suggest we sit down, have a cup of tea and have a chat about darts?" He wrote back saying, "I see no point in the meeting." I wrote back saying, "I will now fuck you …"'

From the end of the 1970s to the middle of the '80s the darts juggernaut just kept on trucking and became a multi-million-pound industry, attracting millions of television viewers and tens of thousands of spectators at the events, all supported by a highly profitable industry of darting merchandise that enabled the consumer to play along at home. Right at the top of this pyramid stood a whole raft of brands wanting to shill their assorted wares (tobacco, DIY, cars, holiday camps, breweries) off the back of the popular sport of darts. What had started as a pub pastime was now a mainstream sport where local heroes could quickly become national superstars, but what was unique was that these men were totally different from anyone who had come before. They had all stepped out of the pub and into the spotlight. They were regular blokes who just so happened to be world-class darts players.

One such bloke was the late, great David 'Alan' Evans aka The Rhondda Legend aka Evans the Arrow from the Rhondda Valley aka

Rhondda Fats, who was one of the first superstars of darts. He of the 'Alan Evans Shot': finishing on a triple bullseye to check out on 150. He who started out as a darting prodigy at his local, then played and slayed throughout the Rhondda Valley (as his nicknames suggests), quickly becoming a household name as his fame spread across Wales, where they love nothing more than a home-grown legend.

'He would say what he was going to do – and then he would do it.' John Lowe weighs in with a testimony. 'I saw him play an exhibition and he said he was going to hit twelve 180s that night. And he hit twelve 180s before the last leg!'

Alan shot to UK-wide fame after he appeared in the first televised final of the 1972 News of the World Championship (at Alexandra Palace) flying the flag for Wales and dressed in a red and white tam-o'-shanter, a 1970s red footy shirt and a pair of voluminous flares topped off with some very clunky Cuban heels. When he won the 1975 Winmau World Masters, which also happened to be the first televised darting event on the BBC, he jumped around the stage with joy, waving a massive leek, which probably annoyed the crusty old men who ran the corporation. You can hear them grumbling, 'What the Dickens is that Welshman playing at?' as they sat in their club peering at the spectacle on a tiny TV screen. Alan went on in the same year to clean up and take home the World Masters title.

'Evans's delicate style, poised like Eros, was in marked contrast to his chunky appearance,' Sid Waddell recalled in *Bellies and Bullseyes*, of Alan's distinctive playing style. 'There was a balletic quality to his throwing action and he held his arrows like a surgeon about to slice – ever so delicately. His dark Celtic features snarled at a miss, soon to be followed by a war whoop that Cochise would have been proud of when he shot well. He leapt in the air giving Denis Law-style salutes to his fans [who] mobbed him off the oche.'

After winning the double, Alan went professional. At the time, he recalled how he'd been on the dole for long periods, but when he could he worked as a brewery drayman. 'After we'd put the barrels in the cellar, they couldn't get me off the dartboard!' he explained. 'I wanted to be a footballer and had trials with Cardiff City, but rheumatic fever put paid to that dream when I was sixteen. But I am now at the start of a new dream.' This showed his followers that darts wasn't just something you did in the pub, it was something that you could earn a decent living from. Alan was the player who turned darts into something aspirational; a pursuit that could actually better your life.

'I get well paid for my exhibitions so I can afford to pay a driver every week. I like a few pints and sometimes I have more than a few, and then you've got the breathalyser coming into it so, some people might think it's for show – but it's not really,' Evans went on the record back in the day, sat in the back of his mauve Daimler Sovereign whilst being driven by his chauffeur. On his way, no doubt, to play a match over a few pints. There is some great footage of the little fellow walking up onto the stage of a working men's club in the valley, sucking down a pint in a couple of steps, which is what they used to call 'warming up'.

Without his darts in his hand, he was an unlikely heart-throb: rather greasy hair, a pimply complexion and the most off-white teeth you'll ever see on a world champion. But the thing about darts heroes is that they often look like the people who they play for, the people who worship them, and it was these people who paid 50p a pop to watch Alan play in cinemas, bingo halls and working men's clubs around the country. He did a five-month tour of Butlin's holiday camps, and averaged eight 180s a week.

When you number-crunch his statistics, it becomes apparent that Alan never really won as many title matches as he should have for someone of his skill level, but he did get to lose a charity match to Muhammad Ali. Okay, so the odds were stacked against Alan as he was only allowed to hit trebles, with Ali finishing on a bullseye, but he still stood shoulder to shoulder on the oche with the world's greatest.

But then, at the height of his success, it all went a bit wrong for Alan. During an international match, whilst playing for his beloved Wales, he apparently called an English match official a 'smarmy cunt' – for which he received a twelve-month suspension from playing. This must have had a major effect on his career, and even though Alan made a valiant comeback after the ban, reaching the semi-finals of the World Championship a couple of times, he never won another major championship. He does, however, hold the record for the highest-ever score on the charity round of the cult TV show *Bullseye* – 401 (which they kindly doubled up to £802). Once on a tour of Scotland he finished with three bullseyes eight times in one match. Who says he died without reaching his potential?

'From when I first met him at Tonypandy Working Men's Club in 1970, I knew he was special. His darts were awe-inspiring. He made people aware of the game and he loved to be in front of the crowd – especially if they were Welsh,' remembers Leighton Rees, 1978 World Champion, and fellow teammate on the notorious Wales international darts team.

As I was roaming around a BDO event at Lakeside (venue for the BDO World Championship) one weekday afternoon, I got chatting to an elderly official with some amazing lamb-chop sideburns, who was in charge of the door to the players' bar. I quizzed him about who he thought were the legends of the game. Those who needed to be name-checked.

He told me, 'Leighton Rees was the first superstar of darts. He was the first winner of the Embassy. But if you want to go further back to the first superstar, Tommy Barrett – a Londoner – twice won the News of the World before the BDO was born. Tommy Gibbons – a Yorkshireman – Bill Duddy, a local from here won the News of the World. They were the superstars and they were the originals.'

One of the greatest rivalries in darting history was between Eric Bristow and Jocky Wilson, and a glorious confrontation between the two has gone down in darts folklore. The camera sets the scene: the audience was smoking, drinking, coughing, shouting out into the thick hazy air, their eyes smarting but locked on the tiny dartboard at the back of the minuscule stage, waiting for their gods to reveal their super powers and unleash some arrows.

After slugging it out for a couple of hours, the two players were neck and neck on the scoreboard. The tension could not get any tighter, the arrows any sweatier. Eric stepped up to the oche, scanning the audience with a slight sneer on his face. He checked the board, and threw a dart straight into the bullseye. He repeated this. And again. It seemed as though the darts couldn't all fit into the tiny metal circle slap bang in the middle of the board, but they did, and just for a moment, one looked like it was going to fall out, but it didn't. The crowd barely registered this rather amazing feat. They were totally ignoring his skills, as he was English.

Eric stared out into the haze, made a face, shrugged as if to say 'don't give a toss' and walked over to remove his darts. Then Jocky – as wide as he is tall – lumbered up and took aim without a second thought. His first dart flew straight into the bullseye: bang. Bang. Bang. Three bullseyes in a row, like Bob Marley shooting the sheriff.

There was a moment of calm. A blip on the radar of noise, and then the place went absolutely ballistic. The bomb dropped and devastation ensued. This was an old-school darts tournament in the heart of Scotland, after all; this was back in the day when it was a proper working-class sport for that very reason; this was the real deal, the genesis of what today's game is now. A right rowdy night out that you may never recover from. This was what darts was all about. Heavy, heavy legends playing around the country to crowds who expected to be able to consume as much as those under the spotlight, slugging it out on the oche. Jocky stood there, drinking a pint in celebration and waiting for the place to calm down somewhat.

Eric moved back in position, threw three darts and ruthlessly ended the game on a double ten, and then looked around to give Jocky the biggest smirk you will ever see on live TV. The moment hung for a second but Jocky had no other choice but to smile and stick his hand out, muttering something. If you watch the footage carefully, you can

see Eric pause, wondering if he should demean himself and shake the
proffered hand – because what no one knew was that moments before
the players had been introduced to the roaring crowd, Jocky Wilson
had tried to nobble Eric Bristow.

'Just as I was about to bounce on stage, Jockey took a run at me and
kicked me as hard as he fucking could in the shin. He took about two
inches of skin off my shin. Christ it hurt, so I grabbed him by the throat
and I was going to fucking kill him, but five officials managed to prise
me off, and shoved me onstage into the bedlam of lights, television
cameras and baying crowd – they were Scots, what do you expect?'
Eric recalled in his autobiography *The Crafty Cockney.*

'What did you do?' I blurted, totally caught up in his book, which
I was reading as part of my research, and before, I may add, that Eric
had totally disgraced himself.

'Well, after that I had to thrash the fucker, and when it was all over
and Jocky came over and shook my hand, he told me, "I've got to try
to beat you somehow ..." And after that I had to laugh.'

The next thing they knew, Eric and Jocky were propping up the bar
together, the kick already forgotten. No major beef. No long, drawn-out
feud that would interfere with their playing or their 'career' trajectory.
This is a valuable insight into what makes darts so special. A spot of
casual violence resolved by a brutal thrashing on live TV and then
the equilibrium restored with a pint or ten. In this day and age, with
doping and cheating and scheming in the 'proper' and 'respectable'
sports, I have to salute this honesty, as warped as it may seem.

That clash of the gods took place in the golden era of darts when
millions regularly sat down and watched on television and the
supporting industry couldn't churn out the assorted merchandise
(darts, boards, hats, mugs, cigarette cards, shirts, books, magazines)
quickly enough. It was a time when the BDO tightly regulated and ran
the industry and decided what happened and what didn't – and this
arrow-filled Nirvana seemed like it would last forever.

Darts had travelled far from the first televised matches in the early seventies, but just over a decade later, unforeseen and pretty much unchecked by the BDO, the tide was about to turn. In 1983 the public watched a lot of darts – it was broadcast on both the BBC and ITV – but the knives were being sharpened. The tabloid press began to focus on the huge beer bellies and the hacking coughs that were a result of the drinking and smoking the players liked to do not only whilst playing on live national television (which seems rather unbelievable today), but also after they'd won a tournament – which was much more of the same but on a bigger scale. It wasn't a healthy lifestyle and these men were definitely not the sort of role models that appealed to many sponsors outside the beer and tobacco industries. It certainly wasn't in keeping with the clean happy-family image that the BDO liked to project at every given opportunity. One of Olly Croft's Achilles heels was that he didn't have a clue how imperative the art of public relations and image-control was to a sport under attack in the press.

The relentless bashing in the red tops couldn't have helped, but then a sketch was broadcast as part of the comedy show *Not the Nine O'Clock News* that probably did the most damage to the image and perception of the darts brand. This was the first nail in the coffin. It was of two men in fat suits (Mel Smith and Griff Rhys Jones) dressed in loud shirts who you presumed were going to throw some darts but in fact were drinking pints and shots in order to see who could hold their drink. The winner was whoever stayed on his feet for the longest, not who threw the best arrows. The extreme negative influence of the sketch showed how quickly and easily the chattering classes could be turned against something that they had probably never really understood nor had any real cultural connection to in the first place. The diehard darts fans were upset by the portrayal of their heroes but it was never going to dampen their support; they were used to being ridiculed in the media. But the people in charge of the media chequebooks, and their associated brands, began to see darts in a very different light.

'It goes back to the *Not the Nine O'Clock News* sketch. That hurt darts big time cos it made people think that it was all about being a piss-head,' Russ 'The Voice' Bray told me backstage at the World's.

The second nail in the commercial coffin came on 28 September 1985 when London Weekend Television decided to stop broadcasting *World of Sport*, which carried darts as part of its format, following a dwindling of viewing figures. The third was in 1988 when the BBC cut its weekly darts coverage to just one tournament a year – the Embassy World Championship. A few months later, ITV announced that they would be stopping all darts reportage by the end of the year, and by 1989 there was only one remaining televised darts event on national television. This drastically reduced airtime meant that fewer brands were willing to be part of the sponsorship package, as their total reach had been chopped from tens of millions of TV viewers to the tens of thousands of people who still attended the regular events. The wheels had begun to fall off.

But Croft and the BDO didn't seem overly concerned. They simply re-booted and re-focused on the amateur game, which kept them busy; they were running 800 grass-roots tournaments a year, the majority of them at holiday camps such as Haven, Pontins and Butlin's, for their 30,000 members. Croft still drove round in his Rolls-Royce surveying his empire, but to everyone else it was definitely not perceived as the lucrative and glamorous business it had been just a few years before. The image had crashed almost overnight.

'We were still very busy promoting darts in a big way,' Croft remembers. 'Darts is full of so many nice people. They are really appreciative. It's surprising when you're running a tournament when someone loses in the first round but they still have a lovely time.' It's a point of view that may be heart-warming, but it held little value for the fickle bottom-line obsessed commercial investors, who up until that point had spent a lot of money promoting darts through various brand partnerships. Olly's words were also totally irrelevant to the hard-working professionals of the game who relied on prize money as their main source of income – the majority of which came from sponsors and TV revenue, a purse that was now shrinking rapidly.

The top players had no option but to spend the next few years in the wilderness, travelling around country pubs and clubs playing exhibitions and other low-level tournaments, trying to keep themselves in the public eye, probably playing a lot of dodgy games for very high stakes for the more 'professional' gamblers out there, all without any help whatsoever from the BDO.

'We don't actually employ dart players and we don't owe them a living,' Olly commented at the time in the film *Blood on the Carpet*.

Yet even though the BDO did not 'employ' the players, they did insist that the professionals were not allowed to wear any personal sponsorship logos on their shirts when playing in competitions – televised or not. They could only endorse the sponsors of the BDO. The players were also unhappy with the way they lost their fees to the BDO when playing international matches for the English team. Many meetings were set up where the players aired their grievances with the BDO but nothing seemed to change. The top players must have felt like they were banging their heads against a wall.

Another insulting experience for the professional players was a VHS released by the BDO of the highlights of the 1983, 1985 and 1987 Embassy World Championships. The tape featured Eric Bristow, John Lowe and Keith 'The Feller' Deller, as well as a legendary nine-dart finish from Paul Lim in the 1990 final. The rights of this VHS were always under suspicion, since none of the featured talent was ever offered any kind of remuneration, nor had they signed releases for the use of their images. The fact that the BDO rushed it out, sensing that they were losing their star talents and milking them till the end, says a lot about how they viewed their professional players. It also shows how unregulated and insignificant the rights of the individual players were in the eyes of the BDO.

Player resentment came to a head in 1992 when the world top sixteen, along with their managers, formed a pressure group called the

Darts Council, and approached Olly Croft to ask if he could guarantee more than one TV appearance a year: he couldn't. In response to this they asked if they could stage their own tournaments for TV: he said they couldn't. He didn't even attempt to appease them, which left the players no other option but to set up their own separate organisation – the World Darts Council (WDC).

The last tournament that all the players participated in was the 1993 Embassy World Championship. The newly formed WDC players attempted to walk onto the stage wearing WDC-branded shirts but were stopped by BDO officials and ordered to remove the offending logos before they were allowed to play. This was the last straw for the WDC players, who felt they had no choice but to walk out of the tournament in protest at the appalling way they were being treated.

'Olly's ability, thinking and everything else with the game had become stale,' said Tommy Cox, the founding chairman of the WDC. 'He wouldn't bring in any marketing people, any specialised TV people. He thought that PR was a total waste of money. He didn't try to do anything, nor did he think that he had to justify himself in any shape or form.'

The BDO responded to the boycott by banning every WDC player (which included every champion from 1972 to 1992) from all UK darts tournaments. This was Olly's attempt to break up the WDC and force its members back into the BDO. They also issued a motion forbidding any BDO players entering any tournament that included any of the WDC players, and hastily pushed through a worldwide ban on any WDC players playing abroad at the World Darts Federation conference in Las Vegas. Brutal.

The original rebels' hall of fame:

Phil Taylor
Dennis Priestley
Rod Harrington
John Lowe

Alan Warriner

Eric Bristow

Jocky Wilson

Bob Anderson

Peter Evison

Jamie Harvey

Ritchie Gardner

Cliff Lazarenko

Kevin Spiolek

Keith Deller

Mike Gregory

Chris Johns

(The last two changed their minds after a month or so and went
    back to the BDO)

'We all said that we would stick together, and that's what we did. And
then Olly started his game plan and tried to pick us off one at a time
in order to destroy us, because that's the way he thinks. That's the
nastiness in his head, you know what I mean?' Eric Bristow recalled
twenty-odd years later.

The WDC began their own tournament – the Lada UK Masters,
which was broadcast on Anglia Television in 1992, but it never
gathered enough momentum as a legal challenge from the BDO
stopped it in its tracks. A stalemate ensued as Olly and the BDO
wouldn't lift their ban, and the professionals and world champions
of the WDC wouldn't return to the fold. The legal battle dragged
on for many years with no progress until the two bodies reached an
out-of-court settlement on 30 June 1997. The ethos of the agreement
was 'to promote the freedom of individual darts players to participate
freely in open competition'. The BDO officially recognised the WDC
and allowed the player to choose which body they played for, and
the WDC changed its name to the Professional Darts Corporation
(PDC). A new darting era was born.

'They are my heroes. I love people who gamble everything on the roll of a dice. The vast majority of those players risked their entire sporting existence on the belief that things could be done better. There is a movie just in that. I mean – the pressure they were put under financially, legally – the fact that they were seen as mercenaries, but they had a belief, and that belief today has been repaid in spades.' Barry Hearn again.

Those who take risks reap the rewards.

'Oh, it was a risk all right. We could have lost that court case – all of our names were on it – we would have paid out a lot of money. They tried to stop us earning a living and that was never going to happen,' Keith Deller tells me when I track him down to his stall at the World's, where fans can get a photo taken with him for twenty pounds.

As I begin to write this book during the summer of 2016, darts has surpassed the popularity it held in the mid eighties and is on course to hit a new high. The darts are coming.

'The range of events and the diversity means that it's near to its peak,' said Leon Davis, sports management lecturer at the University of Northampton. 'They need to make sure that the management have got a good strategy, so they don't confuse the fans with too many tournaments so they don't know what they are watching. That happened in the eighties. Also the nature of the actual players is not unfashionable any more. And as quickly as the Bristow–George final happened (the first World Championship final to really capture the public's imagination and pull in some serious viewing figures – the gaucheness of darts epitomised through Bobby George's jewellery and sparkly shirt) and the Smith/Jones sketch came out, it was already starting to seep in – the pot-bellies, not really athletes – it's not really the case any more. It's still got those connotations, but the management work well to make sure at every event the fan wants to go back next year. They're not confusing the fan.'

So to kick off my adventure through darts I thought I'd better invest in some arrows of my own (I reckon the first rule of darts is that you need some to actually play with). Choosing darts meant choosing a set endorsed by a player, which also worryingly meant choosing a governing body of the sport.

By the 2016 season, darts was still firmly split down the middle: a divided entity. The PDC has become the big time, with matches shown on Sky, tons of flash and some serious prize money. The BDO is now lovingly referred to as the 'grassroots' of darts, i.e., no money, no one watches it, but on the upside it has a totally different look and feel, mostly because it's inclusive and allows both sexes to compete – even if the tournaments are in the arse end of Bridlington. In search of further clarity, I called up my mate Steve Corden, a sports journalist, and asked him what he thought of the different sides to darts, and the current state of play.

'I think Barry Hearn radically changed the face of darts. It used to be seen as drinking and smoking on stage at Lakeside and no one would ever think about the players being athletes. Well, they're still not athletes, but the perception of what they actually do has changed massively.'

'Which is down to how it's framed by the PDC?'

'The rise of the PDC has been just phenomenal. They wanted to improve the sport, to make it better and so they created the premier league of darts, which transformed the landscape because they now play every Thursday night to packed houses all around the country – they even took it to Holland this year, it's a big sport there.'

'What happened to the old fans, then? Are they just sat at the back muttering?'

'They're still there, but they go to Lakeside, which is very different. It's for the people who want to actually enjoy the darts as opposed to enjoy a night out. But the quality of the darts there is not as good as the PDC. It's a very different following, which is very much down to the venue. The PDC is all about the big venues, as Barry has almost tried to re-create that stadium rock feel, whereas Lakeside is that intimate smaller gig where you can interact with the players on the stage as you're never that far away. It gives you the feeling of low-ceilinged, smoke-filled rooms – the traditional home of darts. The kind of darts that has been played there for years.'

'The old school of darts. That's the bit I like,' I reminisced, getting somewhat caught up in the romance of it all.

'Barry moved it away from all that and – somewhat – turned his back on it. If you went to both World Championships you'd have two very different experiences, and I don't think there's much of a crossover, as the markets are very, very, different. The only similarities are that they're both around Christmas …'

Steve's insight made me realise what I had to do: I had to immerse myself in both the PDC and the BDO and play as many people as I could (both professional and amateur), thus demonstrating that darts is still the game of the people – the everyman. And what better way to prove this, I thought, than if a bloke like me with a three-arrow average of (currently – watch this space) 37 who hasn't played in years can get up and play some of the greatest players out there. This will most definitely push me to improve my game, and will also show that there is hope for everyone out there who holds a darting dream.

Steve went off to do some proper work, leaving me thinking that darts is such a polarising sport, even from the inside with the amateur BDO vs. the professional PDC – as well as from the outside, where it's not seen as a real sport by those who simply don't get it.

The burning question is, which organisation is the one for me. Did I really have to pick a side?

'Not many people do both sides. They choose. Some want the hype, the half-naked ladies and all the alcohol – and then there are the others who come to us, who just want to see a good game of darts …' Sue Williams, Chairperson of the BDO, tells me on the phone after I call her up to see if I can get some press access. I also need to keep the BDO firmly on side as they run all the amateur matches, into which

I will be throwing myself. I had to start getting my personal game of darts out of the gutter.

So as I set out on my quest into the wonderful, misunderstood, divided, exciting, Anglo-Saxon, raucously wide and wild world of championship darts I wrote a list of the tasks that would make up my quest:

Task 1: My journey has to take me from being a non-player to playing a game of 501 with as many champions of both the BDO and the PDC as I can.

Task 2: To document the lives of the gods of darts: superstar players and hardcore fans – both living the darts dream.

Task 3: To discover and document the rise to fame of the next legends of darts.

So, dearest reader, sit tight as we ride off into the darting sunset, this one's going to be a little different – for both you and me.

King ADZ, Barnet, May 2017

Interlude #1 – The reality is that I'm shit at darts

When I was a teenager in the eighties I used to play darts fanatically and yet, to be frank, I was pretty shite at it, even though I put in a decent number of hours at the oche. In the end I could just about hold my own in pubs (marginally better than I could hold my drink) but that never mattered as it was the only sport that I ever enjoyed playing – I could smoke and drink and talk absolute bollocks whilst playing a game of round the clock. But then life got in the way and I travelled the world, got married and helped bring up my two kids – who have now left home. It's been thirty years since I picked up a set of arrows, let alone bought some custom flights to mark them as my own. I am laying my truth on the line here, hoping you are a visionary and trustful reader, as the bare bones of the matter is that right here, as things stand, I am absolutely rubbish at darts, and this needs to change.

One of the murkiest sides to darts has to be the world of arrow sponsorship, as that too seems to be a divided business, but also a pretty lucrative earner. Winmau are the sponsors of the Lakeside World Championship and sponsor the top BDO players; Target produces the very reasonably priced £19.99 Phil Taylor set, as well as backing the 'upsetter' himself, Keith Deller. I get sucked into the interweb for almost an entire afternoon, perusing the options for darts equipment and merchandise, and have to fight the urge to buy some seriously questionable items. One thing is for sure – there is some significant money being made.

At one point my wife comes into my office and I quickly hide the browser, so embarrassed at what I have collected in my basket. This pause gives me time to reflect on some choices made in haste, and when she's mooched off I get rid of a couple of items: a Piranha shirt in violent green and a Cool Play Breathable grey and orange shirt XXXL with some very large breast pockets. There are some even worse crimes against fashion in the sales section of the sites I find myself trawling. Every shirt is open-necked and offers no top button (which instantly rules me out as I can only wear a shirt if it's properly buttoned up to the top), and nearly all favour zips – which are in direct contravention of the Geneva Convention. When it's time for me to choose, in the spirit of fairness, I go for a set of Deta 'Dark Destroyer' Hedman darts (BDO) and some Devon Petersen South African flag flights – and as soon as PayPal has done its thing, I begin to look forward to combining them into a custom mutation that will miraculously improve my game. Now all I have to do is put in some hours in order to get my skill level up.

I wander around my neighbourhood to find somewhere to practise. There isn't much choice as I live in the cultural Bermuda Triangle of East Barnet Village, Cockfosters and New Barnet. Between a rock, a hard place and a slab of polished granite. East Barnet has seen better days, with a kosher butcher and a very typical cobbler / luggage / key-cutting shop run by an Alexei Sayle look-a-like, which tells you a little about how wonderfully strange it is. There's a big old carvery-style pub but when I wander in I can find no sign of a dartboard.

'You got a dartboard in here?' I cheerfully ask the barman. His blank stare tells me all I need to know.

Cockfosters is the heartland for the aspirational and predominantly Cypriot community who have 'made it' and moved out of some of the less well-off areas (do any such places still exist?) of London to suburbia where they own a 1950s semi with a Range Rover and a convertible for the wife parked on the expensive brick drive that's lit at night by the sunken xenon lights. The vehicles are white, the lights are that weird science-fiction blue, the houses were once your average commuter-belt semi but have been extended every which way and go for a million or two. Good luck to them, I reckon, but it's hardly an incubator for darts – if such a thing exists. The row of shops near to Cockfosters tube is ram-jammed with Mediterranean restaurants that are supposedly frequented by the Arsenal football team; the training ground is just up the road. On a Friday and Saturday night it's like a badly parked car show, complete with sculptured haircuts bobbing around.

So I walk up to the other side of town, to New Barnet, which is most definitely positioned towards the 'more real' end of the scale, but still not Beirut on a bad day. Opposite the Sainsbury's there is a pub called the Lord Kitchener. It's the kind of pub where men – always men – queue up outside smoking fags (vaping still hasn't reached EN5) and eating bags of chips whilst waiting for the place to open, which should have tipped me off – and it's into this old-old school pub I venture with my darts clutched tightly in my hands.

The place isn't full enough to go quiet as I enter, but the first thing I spot is a giant St George's Cross flag hanging above the bar, which indicates my quest to find a board might have been fulfilled rather quicker than I first thought, as this appears to be a very English pub, and darts is a very English game.

Julio Iglesias' 'Begin the Beguine' is playing on the video screen, and in direct and perhaps ironic contradiction to the straight-up Brexit vibe the place gives off (it's very white and very right and seriously blokey), the first game I play in a proper boozer is against Jay, a Filipino care worker who has wandered in to practise his game. He is dressed head to toe in black, from Converse to condom hat, and he turns out to be a blinding player.

At least Jay is kind. He lets me play a straight game of 501 as the pub team rules are 'double in and double out' (start and end on a double), which would mean I most likely wouldn't even get started. Then I have problems working out my score as my mental arithmetic is up there with my darts, and Jay has to shout it out each time. I throw my arrows badly and my mind goes blank when it comes to adding that shit up and it is so fucking embarrassing, it's like being back at school trying to write something on the blackboard with chalk, except this is in a rowdy-assed right-wing pub and because Jay is obviously helping me with everything, a few people clock this and begin to watch my humiliation.

'Who's the four-eyed retard?' I hear someone growl. This is the moment I know not to turn around and scan the bar. You are obviously judged on darts skill in this place. We play on and then a miracle happens: I get a treble 20. The first one I've probably ever got. Jay is almost as relieved as me that I'm not hitting the low numbers and is like 'yeah!' and I'm happy but then after pulling my darts out of the board I turn to see a row of faces at the bar looking at me with disgust. Somehow, I'm the one letting the place down, or perhaps it's because I'm getting my ass handed to me by a Filipino, who by now is on the purple Bulmers, and I don't blame him. Or maybe it's my arithmetic skills that are winding up the locals. One or the other.

Jay beats me by a mile each time. The worst is when I have 20 left and I try to go out on a double 20. 'You want double ten,' Jay kindly points out. I've one dart left and it misses the board. Of course I want a double 10, I was just having a moment. Probably the fifth pint of shandy didn't help.

Jay goes out on a double 13 and I shake his hand. 'You off?' he asks and he's not being sarky, he genuinely wants to play more darts, but I just can't face it, nor the chatter and the eyes from the bar.

'I gotta go, mate. Thanks for the game.'

'I play here every Friday for the team.'

'And how often do you practise?'

'First time was today!'

It's as I wobble home in the horrible suburban dusk that I realise that I'm completely and utterly shit at darts, and even if I wasn't, I won't be playing for the Lord Kitchener, or even using it as somewhere to practise anytime soon.

CHAPTER TWO

THE BDO

'The Lakeside Country Club is renowned as one of the foremost
entertainment hubs in England, graced by local and international
celebrities and royalty.'

Lakeside Country Club website

Hallowed ground for fans of the BDO who (to quote Wolfie Adams)
'are absolutely brilliant. They give good order when the darts are
on and they have a great day', is Lakeside Country Club in Frimley
Green. I've never been to a country club, so I am eager to kill two birds
with one stone.

My initial reaction when walking into my first official BDO event
at Lakeside – The BDO/Winmau Youth and International Play-offs
and World Masters – is one of a warm fuzzy nostalgia for the seventies,
my first decade. The words 'TV entertainer' spring to mind, closely
followed by 'nightly cabaret dinner dance', and then 'what the fuck?'
because there is no press pass waiting for me. Unperturbed I tell the
lady I am a journalist on official business (I make a quick executive
decision not to waste time explaining that I am writing a book), which
prompts her to ask me a question 'that only someone from the press

world would know': the maiden name of the chairperson of the BDO, which is her official email address. After I answer correctly, she leans to one side and shouts to someone behind me: 'Wayne!! Wayne!!! This man's press! Let him in!!'.

I wander across the faded carpet of the once-grand foyer, and Wayne nods and gives me directions to the press room backstage – which is basically across the main room and through a black door to the left of the stage.

'Cheers, Wayne!' I quip – and into the world of the BDO I head.

The Main Cabaret Suite (its official title) of the Lakeside Country Club is a huge split-level ballroom-esque entertainment venue straight out of the late seventies/early eighties that hasn't been done up since. Burgundy, ochre and green are the predominant colours, all muted somewhat by the rough hand of time. During the BDO events they manage to cram in 2,000. Huge Cinderella-style chandeliers hang down from black hexagonal shapes cut in the ceiling over many circular tables and a sunken dance floor, neatly surrounded by wrought-iron railings and a number of steps. This place was obviously the height of sophistication when it was originally constructed, but these days it's just rather bizarre, like there's been some glitch in time, and even more surreally I soon discover, the Lakeside Country Club is the only major dinner-dance club left in this country. Who'da thought it? I 'm here for the World Youth finals, which are pretty much self-explanatory, and exclusive to the BDO.

'I get club owners ringing up asking – you got a fucking oil well under your club? We're still here because of the way we operate: no borrowing allowed on the company,' Bob Potter, OBE, the owner, tells me sometime down the line when we meet in the ritzy, glitzy showbiz backstage area.

I wander back out to see that the place is flanked by an L-shaped bar (manned by the only black people in the place), and spread across this land of sparkling lights are thirty-odd dartboards – five in a row – erected like voting booths, and a helluva lot of youths throwing darts.

There are thirty games going on at once, and the protocol is that the loser stays on to score the next game. On the main stage is a rather sorry-looking oche with a kind of arrow that points to a hole where the official dartboard will be placed once the people in the room have played enough games and eliminated most of themselves like a snake eating itself, and the important games begin.

After closer inspection, I discover that the onstage TV set is literally held together with gaffer tape.

I wander about and spot a teenage girl with 'Dart Bitch' chopped into her undercut, so I follow her back to a table of Dutch fanatics, all dressed in the regulation black and orange shirt of the 'Nederland Darts Bond'. Dutch is most definitely the second language being spoken in the room. Sadly, once I introduce myself to the group I discover that not all Dutch people speak English, and I then have to try to explain that I'm not actually stalking their fifteen-year-old daughter but would like to interview her, and not just about her interesting hair cut either. They just shake their heads. I walk away with my tail between my legs and sit down at one of the neighbouring tables where I start chatting to a guy from St Helens (whose accent is so thick I wonder if I'd be better off with the Dutch); he has brought his son here to play darts.

'Does he want to play professionally?' I ask.

'He's just started an apprenticeship as an electrician and likes earning money so I don't think he's bothered about sitting around all day at home pretending to be a full-time darts player.'

'How did he get on?' I ask, referring to the qualification games that are taking place.

'He lost the first match. He was nervous, which is strange as that has never been a problem.' This is the first mention of one of the most important elements of darts – the mental game.

We end up chatting about the difference between the PDC and the BDO and I'm surprised to hear such a quick denunciation of Olly Croft.

'He was stubborn and stuck in his ways. He refused to move with the times.'

'Two words: Barry Hearn,' I fire back, with my new-found knowledge.

'Precisely. He saw what was wrong and fixed it.'

Keith 'Crazy' Carter walks past, his moniker plastered over the back of a shiny black polo shirt. I can't help wondering who gives these people their nicknames: Keith looks like a Northampton accountant. Another shirt announces that the 'Bitch is Back' and then I spot a woman sat at one of the cabaret tables reading a Dorling Kindersley equestrian book entitled *A Balanced Horse*. These are all vital clues to help me build a broader profile of exactly who I am mixing with in the Lakeside Country Club at the tail end of 2016, and then I meet Aneesha Mehda – a very together and bespectacled eighteen-year-old Indian girl who has just flown in from Kolkata with her mother.

'You're not the average dart player!' I joke. 'Do they even play darts in India?'

'You would have thought that but it's rapidly gaining in popularity.'

'It's a rather colonial sport!' I have to slay the elephant in the room, to which she laughs. 'Can I interview you?'

'Sure, but please let me play first!' she replies and we promise to catch up later.

As you might expect, there isn't a great deal of wealth on display at Lakeside. Even the Dutch who have forked out a little more to get here are not the tawdry kind, and they're the second largest demographic here, but despite their numbers, it is a darting lady from Iceland who I get chatting to, as we watch her son getting knocked out by a tall Scottish lad egged on by his loud proud Scottish fan base.

'He likes the multiplication!' she tells me. You couldn't make this up. 'He started playing with his grandad and then asked us to put a board in the garage.'

The boy in question has tears in his eyes as he walks over to score the next game, and I instantly feel myself welling up as I too am caught in the absolute drama unfolding in front of me. I take a couple of deep shuddering breaths and head for the bar to wait for the kid from Iceland to finish scoring.

Alex from Grindavík is twelve and has only been playing darts for a year. 'It's fun to make the calculations,' he tells me as I tuck into a pint of Holsten Vier (who turn out to be the only sponsors of the event).

'Considering you've only been playing for such a short time you're fuck-err-really good,' I autocorrect – he's a sweet lad who doesn't really need me adding to the sorrow of his defeat with some industrial-grade language.

'I would like to play professionally.' He nods. 'My favourite player is Adrian Lewis …'

'Do you like [World No. 1] van Gerwen?' I have to ask.

'No.' And he means it. I don't need to ask twice.

'The BDO is really on its last legs. The prize money they go for is absolutely awful,' said Keith Deller aka The Milky Bar Kid, when we met at the World's. 'Bob Potter has to save them all the time, cos no one else will! Why do you want to sponsor an event when you got all the best players in the world playing at Alexandra Palace? Richard Ashdown (BDO darts presenter) always goes: "Welcome to the home of darts." Well, that's not the home I want to go to!'

Most people who pay the £20 or so for a weekend of BDO are hard-working, British working-class families who like to play, watch and consume darts. On first inspection, their image may need a little polish to bring back a bit of the shine, but perhaps that is where the secret to its longevity lies? The most accurate summation is to compare any moment at Lakeside to a Martin Parr photograph of a frozen Thursday in December somewhere on the periphery of the M25 or M6 or M62. It's a really interesting glimpse of a slice of life that rarely gets seen by more than a few diehard fans. And it's the polar opposite of the manufactured entertainment the majority of the nation is force-fed each and every Saturday night on the idiot box. It's like the BDO is still shot in 4:3 when everything else is 4K HD, and I know which one I prefer.

In order to really understand the BDO I needed to visit one of the founding fathers of darts, the man who took an unorganised working-class game out of the pub and turned it into an international multi-million-pound sporting and entertainment phenomenon – and upset a few people along the way ...

When he first opened the front door I was slightly taken aback at how completely and utterly knackered Olly Croft looked, but then I remembered how long he had been around, and that he had taken a fair bit of battering from an assortment of foes over the years. I followed him in to discover that his lounge looked like it hasn't been updated since that meeting forty-three years ago and looks as tired and worn as the man himself; the once-fancy white bar looked like a faded smile and as he flopped back down into his favourite armchair, Olly looked like he was not very well at all. I asked him if he was okay to do the interview and he waved me away with a laugh and a cough, as if to say, the bastards haven't got the better of me yet!

Olly Croft, OBE, still lives in the house that was the location of the famous meeting on 7 January 1973 at which the BDO was formed. It's a typical three-bedroom house in Muswell Hill that has been extended several times to its maximum square footage.

The walls were covered in family and BDO photos and memorabilia: a photo of Olly and Bobby George, a black-and-white shot of the BDO team on their first visit to the USA, a pendant with the original logo framed on a crest-shaped plaque. A well-shredded dartboard dangled next to the bar (I later learnt that Olly hasn't played since the 1960s). A portrait of Olly and his wife Lorna surrounded by their kids.

The day before the interview I had watched some archive footage of Olly driving around the streets of North London in his gold Rolls-Royce, ruling his kingdom of darts with an iron barrel, and even though he was getting on a bit, he looked bullet-proof; one of those men who seem to age slower than the rest of us. But the moment we meet my heart goes out to him; time has most definitely caught up with him.

'I was going to do a book but then I couldn't remember anything,' Olly told me after I explained (again) why I had come to interview him. 'Will I get a copy of the book?' he asked, and it was then I knew he wouldn't get it or even understand why I'd written it, because of the culture chasm that divides us.

Olly grew up in the north-west London suburb of Kenton and his life took a dramatic turn after his mother died when he was eight and his father remarried a nightmare.

'She beat me, starved me and ended up in prison. I went into a home aged ten.' Which would have been a fucking terrible experience and must have taken its toll, and perhaps had an effect on his ability to trust people. Olly must have been a lively little fellow who couldn't sit still, and by the time he was twenty he was still fidgeting around and not able to just be. Around this time one Christmas his dad went for a beer in the Harringay Arms in Crouch End. He took Olly with him, but must have soon regretted the gesture, given that Olly didn't drink or smoke. 'I had nothing to talk about so I walked up and down the road, came back in and spotted a dartboard. I picked up some darts and started to throw them – and I was quite good.'

Olly was hooked and began to play darts every day. By that time he already had his own tiling business, and throwing some darts was the perfect way to unwind after a hard day's work.

'One night it clicked. I was sitting there as captain of the Harringay Arms team and was playing the Three Compasses team. And it just sort of clicked. There was a real interest in darts, no doubt about it ...'

By 1966 Olly had stopped playing and was involved in the organisation of the London Super League, which began with six teams and grew rapidly from there. 'My brain started working – thinking about how I could get more people involved – and BOOM! The next thing I knew I had a new London darts team and we were playing all over the world.'

When Olly examined the way darts was organised around the country he realised that there was no structure; it was all over the shop and no one was taking control. The only national event was the News of the World Championship, and beyond that there were a lot of local leagues, but no central body to keep it all in order and no national league in which every team could play. Olly's team was playing all over England by this time. 'We'd get a couple of coaches everywhere for the weekend – it was fantastic and I knew there was something happening.' Olly began to take control of darts.

'I received a very cocky letter from a very cocky cockney,' Sid Waddell remembered in his autobiography. 'A bloke called Olly Croft announced himself as supremo of London, and indeed England, darts and offered to bring three star players north to show the rest how to play.' Waddell offered another insight into how driven Olly was in his quest: 'He told anybody who would listen that he wanted to be the "Alf Ramsey of Darts". His dictatorial attitude to the players when he did become darts supremo was to be at the heart of the dispute that ripped darts apart twenty years later.'

When *Darts World* magazine launched in November 1972, Olly realised that if there was a call for a magazine, then there would also be an appetite for a properly regulated championship. This was the moment when he called up as many contacts around the country as possible and arranged the meeting that created the BDO.

'It took place over there …' Olly pointed to the exact spot as I sat down in his lounge on a big old battered cream leather sofa, a relic from the seventies. 'The table was there with the lads sitting around it …' He drew a shape in the air to lock the position of that historic moment in space and time. 'We had an agenda. The first thing we wanted to do was find a name and a logo. I suggested British Darts – as that was what it was all about, and Organisation as that was what we wanted to do – get organised. I put that to the floor and it went through unanimously and then we ran a competition through *Darts*

World magazine to find a logo: three darts with the words underneath in a scroll, and then we moved on from there.'

The first year they had ten counties signed up and added another ten or so each year until the BDO had sixty-six counties involved. 'I kept pushing, pushing all the time, then in 1976 I came up with the idea of doing a British Masters, we had the magazine, and interest from the USA, Australia, Holland, France, who all wanted to come over, so we decided to change it to the World Masters.'

The next (and probably the most important) step was when Olly got London Weekend Television involved, which was the way for the burgeoning organisation to reach scale. TV was the only way that darts could really spread across the land, and then the world. And once Olly had TV, the sponsors started knocking on his door.

'Phonogram (a record label conglomerate)] put a thousand pounds into it – that was all. The following year Harry Kicks from Winmau invited me up to his place in Suffolk and sat me down with a few sandwiches, and told me he would like to put some money into darts. Well, he put equipment in – stage equipment, electronic stuff – and after we shook hands, anything I wanted I could get.'

The BDO was growing into a national name, and the next vital step in its progression was the move to Lakeside in 1986. Up until that point the World Masters had been played in an assortment of clubs, beginning with the Heart of the Midlands nightclub in Nottingham before moving to Jollees Cabaret Club in Stoke-on-Trent, which Olly described to me as 'a room above a bus station'. Exotic, like. But this is where the story gets a little mangled.

Olly's version of events was that the BDO were looking for a suitable replacement for Jollees, when he received a phone call from Lakeside, so he and Tony Green [sports commentator and TV presenter] went down to Frimley to check the place out. 'Bob Potter was in a fucking hole. He was a scruffy builder. We made sure we had ties on. He told us he would be with us in a minute ...' According to Olly, Bob Potter wanted to transform darts into a collar-and-tie showbiz-type event, and

Olly had set him straight: 'I told him that he won't get that way with the darts.' But the two men got on and, fortuitously, it was at this point in time that the BBC was interested in televising the World Masters event. 'Bob and I shook hands. He trusted me, I trusted him, everything was done fantastically, he remembered everything, we became great friends, well, acquaintances not friends,' Olly told me. But even with the fancy new venue and the broadcast TV deal, it still took some time to gather proper momentum. In fact, for the first couple of years at Lakeside the event didn't attract that many people and while they were shooting they had to keep moving the audience from one side to the other, so it looked like it was full to everyone watching at home.

Bob Potter tells a different version. Here's his side of the story:

'I started working with Olly Croft by accident. I didn't want to do it. He wanted to bring darts down from Jollees in the north where it had gone wrong. It was dying. He pulled in here with Tony Green and they told me that they wanted to bring the darts to Lakeside, as they were never going back to Jollees. I had all the big names from America coming at that time … I said, "Yeah, but we don't do darts. This is a nightclub where you come to wine, dine and dance. Two bands a night on a revolving stage. The floor comes out of the ground, with the big names every week." My secretary – Shirley – a Jewish girl who worked with me since she was fifteen – said to me, "They wanna come in after New Year's Eve. They can't do no damage …" I said, "No, we're not going to have the bloody darts on here. It's a pub game and there will be fighting and God knows what and I don't want beer all over the bloody carpets …" And she never left me alone about it. She said, "We won't be doing anything after New Year's Eve, and we'll have ten days when we will be in darkness, at least try it?" "On your bloody head be it!" I said.

'I gave them a week. And I was hoping that we didn't get any press on this …'

Once the BDO found a home at Lakeside, something clicked in the public psyche and the transition into mainstream entertainment began. Some of this was down to colour television, the use of split screen, and people dressing up at Lakeside because it was a dinner-dance venue and in the bleak shitty days of the 1970s gave darts a touch of much-needed class.

The best way for me to distil what it was like to be right in the heart of darts when it became a national focus would be to take you back to Lakeside and the Artistes' Bar for just a moment.

It's an amazing historic snapshot of everything that was both great (Hale and Pace) and shite (Jim Davidson appears several times in various sizes and assorted points in his life) and even worse (there is still a framed picture of Rolf Harris on the wall) about places like the Lakeside Country Club, places that are being slowly erased from the landscape of England. It dawns on me that this place is a perfect fit for the BDO, and this is why it's inevitable that the two became synonymous. This place is a frozen moment of a bygone time when things were much simpler and the whole of show business was tightly sewn up, just like the darts. The room of stars is a gentle reminder of what the crazy world of darts was actually like at the height of the reign of the BDO. I can imagine Olly Croft wandering about like he owned the joint, surrounded by stars of screen, stage and song, in the bar supping on free booze and hovering a few feet above the rest of the mortals. But little did anyone know about the problems that were looming, brought on by the ever-shifting tide of popular tastes and public opinion. This was a snapshot of the golden, yet ephemeral, age of darts.

According to Olly, the split started when some of the most famous players didn't qualify for the Embassy World Championship at Lakeside. 'Bristow, Jocky and John Lowe didn't qualify ...' Olly recalled. He had an emergency meeting with the event sponsor, Embassy, who knew the power that the superstars held, and the brand wanted to hold a special invitational event which would enable these players to qualify. They wanted to fast-track them in, but it didn't quite work out like that.

'They didn't qualify and what happened then was that they started boycotting. We had a tournament called the British Match Play in Great

Yarmouth, and they boycotted that. One thing led to another and then you couldn't trust them … Then Dick Gates – their manager – got them to boycott different things and it was hard to put things together then. You need to know the players will attend. It became a bit of a mess. They formed their own association, doing different things, but I couldn't help them …' Olly remembered bitterly.

'It must have hurt when the split happened?'

'Eric [Bristow] was like a son to me but it probably hurt him as well. He is the same age as my son and we adopted him and went all over the world together. He was number one. He won everything. We were like a mum and dad to him.'

'Did he have his famous temper back then?'

'He was a terrible man to control …'

'And when the split happened, that family friendship was gone …?'

'We didn't see each other. Last time I saw him was when I went to an exhibition last year. I always talk to him – no problem at all. He's always weary like …'

'Who is your favourite all-time player?' I had to ask.

'Eric,' Olly replied without hesitation.

In 2011 Olly was ousted from his position as Managing Director of the BDO, after many players and officials within the organisation were – once again – dissatisfied with the performance of the existing board of directors. There was particular concern about the lack of televised events and the declining revenue from sponsors. Some things never change. I got the feeling Olly wasn't overly impressed with the current state of the management, but maybe he was just suffering a severe case of Founder's Syndrome.

When Olly Croft became involved in darts, it was a simple pub game and he turned it into a spectator sport, with a surrounding industry worth millions of pounds. Through the formation and development of the BDO, he made players such as Eric Bristow, Jocky Wilson, Keith Deller and John Lowe household names. He worked for the BDO for thirty-eight years and was obviously stuck in his ways somewhat, but one thing is for sure: if it wasn't for his leadership in those early years, darts wouldn't be where it is today and I most certainly wouldn't be writing this book and Barry Hearn and the PDC would not be making so much money.

'The year they didn't want me no more I had three sponsors in line. All three pulled out because they wouldn't deal with them.' Olly set the record straight. He paused for a moment to gather his thoughts, as what he was about to say was probably his last ever official comment about his life in darts. 'Every event. Every sponsor. Every TV company. Every venue. Every PR company – I dealt with them direct. I never had anyone in between at all. On everything. I was dealing with about eleven TV companies. I went to twenty-nine countries with the wife. Close to 200 events I was involved in all over the world. I was well involved with everything, I was never here.' Olly paused for a moment, lost in the memories of his darting yesteryear, before quickly snapping back to the present day. 'That don't happen today. They just sit in the office … They're not business people. I'm not blaming them; it's just the way it's gone …'

Olly's part in the story of darts is far too significant to end up as some Wikipedia footnote, with him sat on a tatty old La-Z-Boy with daytime TV sapping his will to live. My initial reaction was that I was gutted for Olly, but I have no say in this matter, apart from these few words at the end of this story.

'Darts is the mouth organ of sport … any fucker can play …'
My wife Wilma

When I return for the Winmau World Championship a month later I bring my own food as the catering at Lakeside is like a car boot sale and man cannot live by Nobby's Nuts alone – believe me, I've tried. Even though the menu may seem okay on first glance by noon the place already smells like my school canteen where they used to put sultanas in the curry. As I walk in some kind of sing-song is happening – a moment honouring the staff of the BDO past, present and future. I am touched, it's like the end of a long cruise in the Med, or a Holiday Fellowship walking holiday in the Isle of Wight in the seventies where you're just so happy to be in the dry and not halfway up a mountain eating a soggy packed lunch, that you'd gladly join in with the singing.

There are a lot of costumes, but at the BDO it's more like a land girls' hen do in Brighton: RAF airmen and Morris dancers (a personal nemesis for me) and the odd Power Ranger. It's like they are trying but not really giving their all. Phoning it in.

Before I know it I've eaten a packet of crisps and a packet of chilli Nobby's Nuts. That's the drug of choice at Lakeside. That and shite lager.

The catering area is hidden away in a sunken corridor right at the back and when I venture down there I am instantly taken back to Francis Bacon Comprehensive, Marshalswick, *circa* 1980. This is not a good thing and the two black dinner ladies eye me suspiciously after I begin to ask questions concerning the contents of certain dishes on their menu.

The main cabaret suite is half full of darts fans and the diminutive MC in an oversized grey suit – looking like someone doing a Toulouse-Lautrec impression – is already on the stage, hyping the shit out of the raffle, the BDO merch stand (where every shirt has a zip instead of buttons), the charity stall and the impending live-on-the-internet-and-some-crappy-freeview-channel draw to see who plays who in the Winmau World Masters.

The legendary Wayne sorts out my press pass and then the BDO officials cold lamp onto the stage for the official draw – which I watch for a minute before going back to the press room to formulate a plan of attack. My fellow hacks are listening and keeping one eye on the draw as they work. Halfway through there is a roar of laughter outside in the main event and everyone in the room suddenly starts paying attention.

'What the fuck are they doing?' someone laughs. 'Why are they doing it again?'

Turns out that one of the BDO officials on stage has had some difficulty recognising the different numbers – he's been pulling out balls for the draw and misreading them. The show must go on and a few minutes later, when all the officials file in, I hear Sue Williams saying, 'Someone couldn't tell their threes from their fives!'

'I heard they've re-named the BDO the British Dementia Organisation!' some old guy with a haircut like Vincent Price jokes, but no one really seems bothered that they had to do it twice. Maybe they know no one is watching? Maybe all that really matters is the men or women throwing arrows at a board. If something like that happened at the PDC heads would roll.

I spend the afternoon hanging out in the players' practice area and soon I'm chatting with Bob Potter, OBE, the owner of the Lakeside Country Club.

'I was with Embassy and then tobacco advertising was banned and they couldn't do it no more and it was all going to end. Three hours before the deadline Olly called me and said he was going to lose the TV if he didn't find a sponsor. So I spoke to Shirley – she died shortly after of breast cancer – and she told me not to muck about, that we should sponsor the BDO. We didn't want any cowboys coming in and ruining all the work we'd done. And we went from there ...'

One of the other members of the press tells me about how Sue Williams' husband Wayne had told everyone in the press room that he didn't like journalists because they couldn't be trusted, and then started screaming at the TV production crew to get out of 'his office', which offers another curious insight into the current state of the BDO.

On the wall of the Artistes' Bar I spot a signed photo of Frankie Laine, which makes me instantly think of *Frank Sinatra Has a Cold*, Gay Talese's groundbreaking 1966 piece – a brilliant and definitive long-form 15,000 words for *Esquire* magazine documenting his journey to interview the singer. He wrote:

Many Italo-American boys of his generation were then shooting for the same star – they were strong with song, weak with words, not a big novelist among them: no O'Hara, no Bellow, no Cheever, nor Shaw; yet they could communicate bel canto. This was more in their tradition, no need for a diploma; they could, with a song, someday see their names in lights ... Perry Como ... Frankie Laine ... Tony Bennett ... Vic Damone ... but none could see it better than Frank Sinatra.

You could replace the word 'song' with the word 'darts', and the world of the entertainer now seems as alien and archaic as the world of the top-flight dart player *circa* 1980.

'You have to keep professionalising,' said darts academic Leon Davis. 'The BDO is an amateur sport. There are no two ways about it. That was the problem that Olly Croft had, that he didn't move with the times, and just as he supplanted the NDA GB in the 1970s, that ended up happening to him because he wouldn't move with the times because he was still looking at it from an amateur mindset and that business mindset is what Barry brought, is why it's where it is today ...'

In an ideal world (and if I was a professional) this would be the bit where I sum up the BDO in a neat, chirpy paragraph, recapping the highs and the lows and the ins and the outs. The BDO is such a strange beast, one that refuses to die even when it's gasping for air, trying not to breathe its last breath; one that is both loved and hated with such passion that I can't help trying to work out why anyone gives a shit either way.

The fact that Deta Hedman (a very successful and black woman player) was one of the commentators for the World Championship the first time it went out on Channel 4 indicates that someone somewhere is trying to make something new happen, which surely must be an exciting new opportunity for the BDO?

The BDO is a strange fruit. A clockwork orange that keeps on ticking when it should have stopped long ago, at which we can't help glancing from time to time to ask, 'What the fuck?'

Interlude #2 – The lower you fall, the higher you'll fly

My trip to the pub hadn't exactly worked out as I'd planned but when a mate suggested I check out a place called Flight Club, I was all ears.

On first inspection Flight Club looks like the set of an American TV ad for a beer that's trying to shed a conservative image and appear 'cool' and 'down', which is a little strange. On the plus side, Flight Club is clean and neat, everything works, the cocktails are all reasonably expensive, the food is reassuringly pretentious and you're not going to get into a fight if your dart accidentally pings off the board and lands on someone's box-fresh trainer. You can't just turn up and play either, and so whilst booking my oche, I accidentally downloaded the menu and discovered it was the polar opposite of what I imagine any self-respecting darts purist would order at the bar of his or her local. The menu boasts dishes such as baba ganoush with stone-baked flat bread. I'm sure it's pretty tasty in the right circles, but it's a totally alien accompaniment to a traditional game of darts. And what is a popcorn mussel? It sounds like something you'd pull, struggling out of your cinema seat after a Lord of the Rings trilogy all-nighter.

I'm not saying darts shouldn't move with the times. No, what I'm suggesting here is that there is the world of darts, and then there is another place – one chock full of big gangs of office workers on away-days, drinking rosé by the bucket, screaming with joy when they actually hit the board with a dart and it doesn't fall out.

I'm here with my mate Jake Hanrahan – the Vice journalist who was arrested in Turkey on the ridiculous charge of 'aiding a terrorist organisation' after he embedded himself with PKK rebels for a documentary. It's a Friday lunchtime, which is as good a time as any to have a drink and throw some arrows. That's as long as I could book the oche, for this here Flight Club turns out to be a right popular place. Upon arrival an American girl kindly launches into the rules of darts and I have to stop her mid-flow.

'Don't worry – we've played before,' I tell her, with my Lord Kitchener disaster fresh in the back of my mind.

'Okay. You guys are all set then,' comes back the standard brand-training-speak from our new friend, as she hands Jake three arrows.

I pull out my own set and we start on a game of 301 with my first dart missing the actual scoring part of the board, but landing very near to the number one.

'Fucksake!' is my standard reply.

Jake guffaws. 'I was worried you were going to kick my ass, but now . . .'

'Just warming up, as you will see . . .' I hit a 5 and a 20.

'Looks like it's been longer than that.' It's Jake's turn and all three of his darts fail to score. For once, I say nothing; revenge is a dish best served cold, and all that malarkey.

Jake is much more than just a journalist. When I met him he was a bare-knuckle boxer who needed a bit of a leg-up into the world of writing. He contacted me about doing a piece on the world's most notorious art smuggler – who I am also pals with. Jake looks like a rougher, tougher Jack O'Connell, but without the Hollywood polish, and twice as street. He has been in some scary situations – the height of which must have been two weeks in a Turkish prison.

'It was a fucking nightmare! Solitary was full so luckily they put me in with my producer.'

It's at this moment that a big gang of City boys pour into the place with much bluster. It's Friday arvo, after all. I order my first pint and Jake goes for a whiskey sour, and we play on, still under the sad pretense that we're 'warming up', which is just a weak-assed way to say we're still undeniably crap. Then we have a little look at the menu. What to eat? We're both starving but as I've mentioned, the menu is pretty out there. After much debate we settle for a 'sharing paddle' of pizza – maybe after we finish it we can go down the street and join the hipsters playing table tennis?

And we play on. I win the first round, Jake the second with a very fluky bullseye, which he insists on photographing.

I look around to see some retro photos of Eric Bristow, Jocky Wilson (I love the fact that he was a miner from Fife who became World Champion – only in darts!!!) and John Lowe, all arranged very neatly on a wall, our benevolent patron saints watching over us. I make a silent plea for some divine intervention but get totally blanked. My darts are not good.

'So when did you last play darts?' I enquire casually, attempting to hide my not-so-secret competitive streak.

'God – probably at my youth club, when I was about twelve or something.'

'And what did you think when I told you where we were meeting?'

'When you said Shoreditch I thought, Fuck me, this is going to be some poncy affair. Don't get me wrong, this is fun, but I can't imagine that people who play darts from where I'm from would enjoy it.'

'Kettering?'

'Yeah, the only place you're gonna see darts there is in a bit of a dive, where people still smoke inside, and spill their beer ...'

'Which isn't necessarily a bad thing – rough doesn't always mean shit. But in the media, darts never gets a fair lick of the stick, does it?'

'No, it doesn't. It's a hard one. If you look at a proper athlete you know they've put the work in, their body looks amazing. Then you look at the kind of bloke that plays darts at world-class level, and it's like he's doing twelve pints a night with pork scratchings whilst he's playing, but who's to say he's any less skilled than anyone else?' Jake has a point.

'It's not as "sexy" – not the sort of thing that carries across so well visually, is it?' I add.

'I think it's good to see darts on the telly. It doesn't look or feel like it's come that far out of the working men's club.'

'What does Vice make of darts?' I ask.

'People tend to look at Vice and think it's wanky-wanky, but it's not. There is a lot of good work going on. Vice would look at darts and say, "That's really interesting. A Jamaican-born female darts champion – that's different." But I'd say that there is this weird turning of the tide – especially amongst the middle-class kids where they're trying to play working class; trying to play a bit rough, as it's actually cool. You will see former middle-class lads with pints and cigs wearing Lacoste giving it "woahay!" That's cool for them now – but if someone brought darts back for them on a Friday night when everyone's dib-dabbing and taking their e's wearing Supreme – they'd love it.'

And this is where we run out of time with our booking. The clock pings and my £15 is all used up and the screen goes blank and a different helper morphs into view asking if we want to move to the bar or just settle our bill. Jake has to get back to Vice HQ and I have a train to catch to go north. As we walk out of Flight Club I realise that the place has nothing to do with the real world of darts. It's a bit of a laugh and a good way for a lot of people to spend an afternoon, written off as 'team building', but it has enabled me to get my arm back in without too much shame. By the time we leave, the place is full of people who are well on their way to being wasted, which ensures that they are even worse with the arrows than I am. A suspect step in the right direction. Maybe I could use this place as my secret practice base? I'm sure Jake won't mind coming back for some more.

CHAPTER THREE

THE PDC

'The difference between the two parties – and this is no knock to the BDO – they've got a very experienced businessman – Barry Hearn – who's gone through snooker, gone through boxing, and when I say through, he has literally ...'

Trina Gulliver, MBE

Wind back to the year 1997 on a cold December night deep in the dusty no man's land that is known as the Arterial Road, a sliver of tarmac off the A13, just to the east of the Thames on the borders of Greater London and Essex. A sleek, expensive car rolled into the already overloaded car park, looking very out of place in the industrial surroundings, and parked up. A figure got out and attempted to get into the Circus Tavern – which on that night was the venue for the Red Band PDC World Darts Championship – as quickly as he could. It was cold, dark and late. He was there on a whim; as a favour to somebody. To be honest, he wasn't sure what the fuck he was doing there but as soon as he got inside that all changed.

'I walked in and there they all were, doing what I loved to do: watching some quality sport, having a nice bit of liquid refreshment, smoking – as I used to in those days – and having a bit of a gamble.' Turns out that the man was Barry Hearn, working-class sports evangelist and probably the most astute mind in the business.

Once he'd wandered around the rather seedy venue (most nights it's a lap-dancing club), Barry turned to the bloke who'd invited him to come down, and told him: 'I can smell the money.' Everywhere Barry looked he could see people having a great time and being entertained. 'There was no pretentiousness about it whatsoever.' And it was at that very moment, twenty years back, that Barry's adventures in the world of darts began. His driving motivation? He 'can't stand snobbishness in sports'.

Today, Barry is the chairman of the PDC and I'm sitting in his Brentwood headquarters on top of a hill overlooking the City of London, in what was once a very swish Georgian drawing room, which would not look out of place in a high-end costume drama, the sort we both avoid like the plague.

'Do you know what's beautiful about darts?' Barry asks me as we sip our builders'. 'It's a complete reversal of everything we have been brought up revering in this world – it's so bloody ordinary. It's played by ordinary people with extraordinary ability. But to a Premiership football player it's a subculture. It's quite bizarre, I've tried to analyse it because my life is all about logistics and analysis – why do people like something? How can I help them enjoy it more? Darts exemplifies all of that, and I still don't understand it. People will say to me, "How have you done it?" And I've never ever been able to give anything other than a simplistic answer about market research and target market and changing trends and younger demographics and all that kinds of stuff. There is a whole social structure built around darts that people miss out on, because it's a throwback to – in a way – old community and old values. Even though it's a different audience watching it. It's not the Wheeltappers and Shunters anymore – on the face of it, it's a major international sport, with big prize money, huge egos, but it still retains that ordinariness.'

What he is talking about is that feeling you get when deep down you experience a true cultural connection, a shared moment of 'I've felt like that', but the secret of darts is that although they appear like those regular blokes you will see down the pub, the players are in fact not ordinary. They have the ability to throw darts very accurately over and over and over and over again under serious pressure. There are three vital elements to darts: skill, mental strength and personality. The skill is about being able to throw amazingly well, the mental strength has to be used to keep your mind in the game leg after leg, day after day, and the personality comes from the sport being born out of a working-class environment – where you have to have a larger-than-life persona to get noticed. A swagger is vitally important for darts players; they have to be able to connect with people, and that's where the gesticulations and exaggerations and celebrations come from.

'There are no barriers to entering the world of darts,' I tell Barry, pleased that I've had an original and relevant insight.

'You don't have to join a club, you don't have to spend a fortune on your kit, you don't need to be part of any organisation. It's a repetition sport that means no matter how sporty or popular you are, you could still be good at this. And for a lot of kids it almost carries an anti-bullying message: "I'm not comfortable in this environment but I can put a dartboard up in my bedroom and get really good." Today they are coming out of the bedroom and they are taking over the game, and this will pose its own problems because they haven't had the background of the old players ...' Barry enlightens me.

The generation of players who are slaying it now and winning all the prizes won't exist for long. They will soon be replaced, upgraded and, more importantly, beaten by the new breed of players who don't drink and don't socialise. These fresh faces/livers are career players, almost solely in it for the money, and because of this, they will be technically better than their forbears, but more than likely they'll lack the magic and entertainment. This is the stuff you can't bottle that makes darts such an interesting phenomenon to follow.

Barry only spends his (by now precious) time on sports that he likes. He doesn't like motorsport and he has no time for tennis. 'It doesn't stop me appreciating the talents they have, but they just don't do anything for me …' And it's this philosophy that has had such an influence on the sports that Barry has got involved in: boxing, snooker, darts, ping pong, ten pin, fishing, poker, pool … Like he said, nothing pretentious, and this is another of the secrets to Barry's success. Be straight up and respect the working classes. Respect the sport that started out in the pub.

I ask Barry about why everything clicked with darts in the 1970s, and why it became so popular.

'TV got into it and found a niche, and the secret was that it was very cheap for TV, but those days are obviously changing now.'

'So it was just an easy and cheap way of making mass-market TV?'

'Yup.'

'So after your little trip to the Circus Tavern, what happened?'

'Back in the day when the PDC went to Sky (as the BDO had the BBC locked up) they were on their knees. It was almost like: "Whatever you want to give us, we've got to take, as there is nowhere else to go." They asked me to look after their TV negotiations because they were getting killed.'

'And how has that changed today?'

'Today the conversation is much more like: "I know what you pay for the Ryder Cup. And I know what you pay for F1, and I know what you pay for football … so explain to me – knowing that my audiences in the championship are DOUBLE the Ryder Cup, are 40 per cent bigger than F1, and bigger than the League Cup final – why aren't you paying me the same money? Am I missing the point here?"'

'Seems like everyone always wants to screw darts on the money?'

'The TV companies don't want to pay the money but at the same time they don't want to lose the product. They reckon that the football fans just subscribe for the football. I'm like: "Do you want to take a chance on that? Because I think that a minimum of 250,000 of your subscribers will fuck off without the darts, and that will cost you £180 million a year. How much do you want to play poker with me?"'

And it's these kinds of insights that play a vital part in the re-education process to take away some of the snobbishness that most people associate with darts. So many people still look down their nose at darts. In business terms most brands totally ignore the opportunity offered by darts. Even just as an export, darts brings in tens of millions of pounds from around the world.

'It's just the narrow-minded and short-sighted brand managers who don't want to accept that it's real. There are a lot of real customers out there who love darts. The data doesn't lie.

'Because working-class people have always been ignored by the media, and by the top commercial people. It's almost … we can't live without them, but we try to ignore them where possible. And the numbers that darts is attracting is making it more difficult to ignore us …'

'So, when you got into a position to make a difference, what did you do?'

'I had a very clear definition of what I wanted to achieve. I wanted volume, a younger demographic, I wanted more females in the audience, I wanted it to be – and not for the wrong reasons – more family orientated, but mainly I wanted it to be a party. I thought darts had come out of a pub; it left the pub behind, but somehow you gotta keep that little bit of pub atmosphere – otherwise you lose what made it great in the first place.'

Barry looked at the customer experience, he made sure the venues weren't over-charging for beer just because they had a captive audience, that the food was – almost – palatable, that the music was something you didn't have to be a trainspotter to remember from your youth, and that perhaps, most importantly, all the players had nicknames and easily remembered personalities. All these ingredients contributed to the creation of a loyal following.

'And it just continued to grow. There is always a certain amount of luck in business and this is no exception. We hit the right time.

There was a change in social trends in the country – whether it was the internet, or perhaps it was the fact that the kids couldn't find a job – all wrapped up in an atmosphere that was so rowdy as sometimes in darts you can't hear yourself think. It's such a contrast to something like, "Shhhh, we're watching the snooker", and the people embraced this contrast.'

For a certain demographic, darts offers a beacon of hope, and entry into the PDC is accessible through the school of hard knocks, aka Q-School. I ask Barry about this – I guess the 'Q' stands for qualifying.

'When we started the Q-School five years ago, I'm looking at scores cos I'm a bit of an anorak. I watch the results of the Q-School come in – and I spot some little fat kid from St Helens creeping up the rankings and he's probably the only kid in his street to have a job. There's no work up there. I don't know whether he got bullied at school cos he couldn't play football and so he went upstairs and practised darts in his bedroom. So now he's eighteen, he's got his tour card – his Willy Wonka ticket – maybe someone pays his entry fee. First event he has a nine-darter and wins £1,500 and he's thinking of getting a drug habit and a Ferrari. Second event he beats five players in the top sixteen and wins £10,000 – changes his whole life in one go. Now he's number 7 in the world he's a premier-league player earning himself £400,000 a year – he could buy his street in St Helens from what he's earning.'

But also what comes with that journey is the recognition, the reputation, the respect – something for other kids to look up to. It's a chain reaction. It's something real and it's something ordinary. And add to that the fact that it's as raucous a night out as you can get and the crowds are playing as important a part of the show as the players.

Talking of the crowds, I ask Barry a burning question. 'What sort of people want to dress up like that?'

'Great big fellas that you wouldn't want to have a row with are walking up from Alexandra Palace dressed in bras and knickers. What other sport in the world has that accessibility to their stars, an almost touch-and-feel in an environment that is so entertaining and coupled

with the fact that it is the only sport that is not visible to the naked eye.
You can be seated in the front row but you can't see the double top –
you're looking at a screen. You could be sat at home looking at the
same screen, why the fuck are you paying 30 quid a ticket? The answer
is that it's a great crack and it's the atmosphere that makes it …'

And with these words, my time with Barry is up. He sorts out my
request for press credentials for the forthcoming season starting in
Wigan the following month and then sees me out to make sure I don't
nick the furniture. As I walk away past his Bentley, he shouts out that I
should 'Go west!' if I want to take a proper journey through darts, and
that we should meet again soon.

THE MEN IN THE SHADOWS

'There were fourteen in the split after the two went back, they
were trying to put tournaments on TV, trying to make it a money
tournament, trying to get a sponsor, scratching to do it. Tommy Cox
and Dick Allix did a fantastic job in what they done. But as soon as
Barry got his teeth into it … I mean Barry smells money – he can sniff
it out from under a stone – Barry is one of the biggest entrepreneurs
you could ever encounter … and once he got his teeth into it and
picked it up and said– this is what we're going to do, he knew the right
people to talk to, the right people to get sponsorship, people were then
jumping to get on the bandwagon …'

Russ Bray, aka The Voice

But what was it that took darts from the greasy environs of the Circus
Tavern to selling out Alexandra Palace twenty nights in a row? What
really happened behind the scenes?

One element in the equation of success is the way that the PDC has
sold itself to the world. It's a slick business with some serious people at
the helm. That is the main difference between the PDC and the BDO,
and you have probably worked that out for yourself by now.

I looked a little deeper into the mechanics.

The PDC has blatantly adopted Americanised sports-marketing concepts – the whole popcorn, beer and hotdogs thing that you get in baseball, American football, ice hockey, the NBA and, most importantly, WWF. But this side of the pond the model relies on selling way more beer, Pizza Hut and Burger King with their events, and this seems to give out the wrong impression to potential sponsors. I looked around at the other sports to see what brands were involved: the national cricket team is sponsored by Waitrose; rugby by O2; and football has become dominated by the unrecognisable far eastern betting sites – you don't get much more mainstream brands than those. Compare them to the brands associated with darts – William Hill, Peperami and Sun Bets – and you begin to see just how darts is viewed culturally. This kind of branding is a cash cow for the PDC but it's also a thorn in its side.

The root of this dearth of decent sponsors has to be the sport's working-class origins, which plays havoc with some of the commercial aspects of the sport and manifests itself in its appetite for fast food, gambling and beer. The PDC may have eliminated the gambling, smoking and drinking from the players but not from the fans, and when the proposition of sponsorship is put to the marketing managers in the board room, they have major trouble getting past this. They just don't get what is happening in cultural terms (which is in reality something that is easily exploited and monetised) and fail to see the real potential; there is a huge opportunity for a progressive, brave brand to step up and fill the void.

Barry told me, 'Where you hit the nail on the head is – it's the perception amongst the power-brokers – why is it, you tell me with the numbers we hit, which are only second to Premier League TV – why are all my sponsors gambling companies? I talked to the sponsor director of the Hong Kong Shanghai Bank – a guy I've known for years, and I said, "You advertise that you are the banker to the people of the world. I've got the sport of the people of the world …" He turned round to me and said, "If I go into my board meeting and suggest darts, I would be out of a job." And that is the perception which I find frustrating in a way, but in another way I almost like it – in the same way as they don't like something that is popular. I like sticking it up people. And then I like them coming to the event.'

One reason darts is struggling to find decent mass-market sponsorship is because it is not fully globalised, yet. Although it has used a lot of Americanised concepts it hasn't actually cracked the American market, and the brands and their custodians know this. All eyes are on how darts gets on with our American cousins.

Back to Leon Davis, my font of deep knowledge: '[Hearn] is up front with what he sells and he sells it cheap. He builds it high and sells it cheap. He makes it available to the consumer. Football went away from that by pricing itself as a middle-class sport. They thought that after Hillsborough, to survive, they had to market it at a middle-class audience and the ticket prices went up a thousand per cent in the space of four or five years for essentially the same brand, just with a different badge. Whereas you or I might look at it from a fan point of view, the PDC are looking at it from a producer–consumer perspective. They're thinking, We need to cater for the VIP consumer and the working-class and it's about offering a range of ticket prices that are categorised these days.'

Two names that kept cropping up during my research are Dick Allix and Tommy Cox, the two men who, with John Markovic, founded the PDC in 1992. Dick states on his website, 'As the fortunes of televised darts dwindled, I created a new company with fellow manager Tommy Cox – the Professional Darts Corporation (PDC), which wrestled control of the professional game from the ineffective governing body.' Both men were successful darts agents and between them they looked after the lion's share of the greatest players ever, and in hindsight it seemed the obvious thing to do. In hip-hop speak they always say 'don't hate the player, hate the game', and this seems a relevant phrase to drop now.

'Dick Allix and Tommy Cox stood with me in shady corners at the early Embassy World Championship and wisely marked my card. They were at the forefront of the players' fight for democracy in the sport and both are good friends.' Sid Waddell, in his autobiography, summed things up.

'The whole reason for darts' existence after the 1970s is television. It's the essential focus,' Leon Davis told me. 'That's why it died. That's why it dipped. That is the point of the split. Barry Hearn was the big catalyst in the late '90s -early '00s, but with any sport, post the '90s, if you don't professionalise then you are not going to get the exposure that you need to survive as a fully professional sport.' We saw it in rugby; we saw it in football and the Premier League. Darts equally had its own revolution of sorts.

One essential point is that Dick and Tommy's timing was spot on with the creation of the PDC, as it coincided with Sky TV claiming a larger audience/subscriber base. After meeting Olly Croft, I was really confused about why he had spent years toiling for the BDO, as he told me he had never made any money from it, whereas the PDC is all about the money. This indicated that Olly was doing it for the power, the control, the position.

Once the PDC started to be broadcast by Sky, the coverage was developed by two producers – Martin Turner and Peter Judge – who had seen what it took in the US to transform sport into entertainment, and allowed a little of it to rub off on darts over here. When you compare what happens at Lakeside to the show at Alexandra Palace, it seems like two different sports. I will leave the last word to someone who has played an active role in the television development from behind and in front of the camera, John McDonald, the face of darts on Sky: 'If you really want to look at the real success you have to give Sky a tremendous pat on the back, as they realised that they needed flags and walk-on girls and fireworks and music and these characters need nicknames just like WWE and all that razzamatazz. But this was all down to the two people who developed it, as it's down to these two guys that made it the show, the carnival/circus that it is today. Barry got involved after seeing one of their shows and then it became the Barry Midas touch.'

One PDC memory that stuck with me was when I was sat in the press room in Minehead Butlin's, during the Cash Converters Players Championship, typing notes, trying to look busy, when I hear someone behind me talking to his colleagues. Turns out that these are the highest of the high – the PDC's directors who have come to monitor everything. They are mission control, and at that precise moment they have a problem with the TV commentator, who keeps referring to Butlin's as a 'big top' live on ITV.

'He's gotta stop saying that. Barry just called up, says it's not a fucking circus.'

I go back to work and a short time later the commentator walks in and is called over.

'You can't call it a big top. Sounds too much like a circus. Call it the Skyline Arena.'

'[so-and-so] keeps calling it that!'

'Well, she's useless and you're meant to be good!' The hand of Barry Hearn is never far away.

Interlude #3 – Rude vibes on a Wednesday evening in Wolverhampton

> *'They're sort of making it more into a sport – more professional, no drinking and things like that. Whereas I do think we're still very old school with that – everyone still drinks, the majority of the players still drink heavily. But I've seen it where girlfriends and drink has affected their play and there have been a couple that were very very good darts players in World Championship finals and the premier league who are gone now and you can tell it's the lifestyle that's affected them.'*
>
> *Daniella Allfree, A-team walk-on girl*

Into the lions' den I wander ... I thought I would walk into the place and the energy would hit me like a train, but in reality, when I get there they are still putting out the hundreds of bright green plastic leprechaun hats (courtesy of the nice folks at Peperami) on the long tables that fill the main floor of the Wolverhampton Civic Hall. I hang around the freezing foyer as the security team is being briefed – are they expecting trouble? I wait for the bloke who deals out the press passes and peer through a porthole into the hall to see a lad in a pair of skinny jeans shaking out the last of the aforementioned hats and tossing them on the tables. It's like a beer keller but with brighter plastic and neon colours and logos – Singha, PDC, Sky, Sun Bets, Peperami. I slope across to the merch stand where the Wolves lass kindly asks if someone is looking after me and I nod and smile like the village idiot and to fill the impending void I ask what is her best seller. I must look like a fish out of water – I certainly feel like one.

'For small, the 180 deely-bopper headband – twelve pounds. For big, the van Gerwen neon green playshirt – sixty pounds,' she answers cheerfully. Showing I care about such details, I check the flights out and just as I'm about to ask if I can try on one of the multicoloured Peter

Wright Mohican wigs the press bloke turns up and asks my name. He scans a list, finds my name and tells me that I'm 'writing a book'. He hands me a small white pass complete with lanyard. I put it on and think, *Now what?* The moment hangs, and then I remember the two magic words that will come in very useful on my quest.

'Where's Dave?' I ask, and thankfully he points me to the back of the hall.

'There's a bloke dressed like me . . .' He fingers his striped silver tie and black mafioso shirt. 'Ask him to send you to the press room.'

I wander past the many bouncers and workers and after floundering about the back staircase for a bit I'm soon in the media room, which is basically a shabby corridor, like a Portakabin on the side of the M25, full of neat young popular guys all enjoying some banter. It's a little like the first day at school (we used to call them 'the lads') as everyone looks over in my direction. By now I must have a huge sign flashing above my head that states 'this guy knows fuck-all about darts', but then Dave the PDC media manager clocks me, stands up and basically puts a magical and metaphorical arm around my shoulder as if to say, he's with me. Which is the nicest thing he could do as I was about to bolt out of there and get myself a green Peperami hat to try and blend in a bit. Dave is honestly (a word that is rarely used in these days of relentless self-promotion) interested that I'm writing a book on darts. He sits me down on a plastic crate full of merch and takes me through everything about the back end of darts from start to finish.

When he finishes, he hands me a programme and schools me about the exact order of what will actually be going down tonight. I mention who I want to interview and he writes their names down on a classic reporter's spiral-bound pad and tells me that there is more chance of this happening if they win – but if they don't the players will be straight out of here as the last thing they want to do is chat to some oke writing a book on darts. Which I get.

'Do you want a tour?' he asks.

'Does the Pope shit in the woods?'

The tour takes me through the Dutch TV 'studio', which is a small room/corridor next door with a backdrop stating 'RL 7 darts' for interviews for the Low Countries. Further down the corridor is the room where the 'walk-on girls' and the MC John McDonald get changed. I know this because there is a scrappy A4 piece of paper with 'Walk-on Girls' in green marker and 'MC JMcD' in red, taped on the door. At this point I don't even know what a walk-on girl is.

Next up is the referees' room and this is when I remember that I am meant to be doing a chapter on those very people and make a mental note to go back and poke my head in. Dave leads me out to the balcony where we watch the fans streaming into the civic hall. There are loads of the big old-school TV cameras on wheels gliding about the stage as the Singha Beer Grand Slam is broadcast live on Sky Sports (as are all major competitions). Then we descend into the VIP bar (where there is an illuminated dartboard and half-price drinks); it is filling up nicely. We keep moving, down down down towards the belly of the beast, past a very thorough female bouncer and into the players' area where there are three boards in a line. I'm not really allowed in but Dave swings the door open with his foot to reveal a miniature (he seems quite far away) grey-haired man throwing some arrows. He's dressed in a blue and white shirt with POWER written all over it, which shares the same design aesthetics as a bottle of White Lightning. This is the first actual time I've seen a professional player in the flesh with my own eyes and after squinting a bit I realise its Phil Taylor, sixteen-time World Champ. To put it bluntly, Phil is the best player there has ever been and probably ever will be. The best of the best.

'He doesn't warm up that much any more as he gets tired,' Dave lets me into a secret. 'But someone like Dobey will come in here and play for a couple of hours …' We creep away and I can hear the noise building in the place. Dave has to run off to solve a logistical problem (Sky TV gave away half a balcony of free tickets to some kids and the security are worried or something) and I slip into the VIP bar and get a pint of Singha for £2.50 (win!), and take it up into the safety of the media-only balcony to watch the action unfold. Remember, this is all new to me.

By now the place is full. The long tables are swarming with brightly dressed people with huge jugs of bright orange lager or two-pint glasses of thick black Guinness. There is a gang of cone heads. A team of really bad Hawaiian shirts. What looks like some Mexicans. I watch a man carrying two massive jugs of lager wearing a shirt that Dave had described earlier as 'Foul Fashion' join several more of the same style of shirt already sat down at their table, all territorial like. He almost spills the lager but that would be too perfect. There is nothing subtle about any of this and when I look it up later Foul Fashion turns out to be an actual brand and not just a casual definition of someone wearing something entirely shit. I spot a group of men and women looking like they've come straight from work, with matching standard-issue navy blue polo shirts with 'players club' on the breast and their name on the back (Gapman, Bart, Maggie, Sparkles, Estelle). The women – who make up about 40 per cent of the audience – are dressed a bit smarter than the men in their glitzy tops and dip-dyed straightened glossy hair, but everyone seems primed for a night of haziness and thorough fun. I sit back and take a sip of very average lager, and close my eyes for a moment … I'm feeling a bit fucked.

And even though I'd love to just sit up in the sanctuary of the media balcony, I force my sorry ass down into the main arena just as the Sky TV feed is about to start and the audience who have clocked this are streaming towards the entrance tunnel. When I get down there, the place is now Babylon. Not the atmosphere but the fact that I am completely out of my *comfort zone, as it's getting more and more rowdy and I am like a minnow in a shark tank. Or a tasty little mackerel. Whatever the metaphor I'm going to get eaten alive if I'm not careful.*

The MC John McDonald wanders onto the stage wearing an electric-blue suit ('I'm only Mr Entertainment, I'm only brought here for my looks really, as you've probably noticed, Adz, the show is basically about me with a bit of darts thrown in!!' he jokingly tells me later) and a very bright smile. There is a dip, a blip, a moment of calm and then the darts theme tune plays – this is the first time I've heard it – and John lets rip:

'Welcome to the Singha Grand Slam of Darts, live from Wolverhampton Civic Hall!'

THE PLACE GOES FUCKING MENTAL.

And I have to try to keep upright as I'm suddenly surrounded by the gang of dartboard-poncho-wearing twenty-somethings who hold up their costumes to make a line of boards, faces hidden by hats tipping down to compete the bullseye. A trompe-l'œil indeed, but I don't really have time to think as it's turned into a bit of a darting mosh pit and I'm struggling to keep my balance.

'What is it that brings you down here on a wet Wednesday night?' I ask a twenty-something woman in a George Michael wig and 'Frankie Says Relax' tee when things have settled down a bit and I've recovered my glasses and got over the fact that I wasn't really enjoying that pint of lager anyway.

She looks at me like I'm retarded. 'The darts!' she shouts as everything steps up a gear and the first player waddles out accompanied by a busty leggy brunette in a sparkly micro-dress whom I assume to be a 'walk-on girl'.

'Yeah, funny.' I bounce back when I realise that she is pulling my leg.

'Dunno what to say roily. It's a bloinding night out,' she tells me in her thick Black Country brogue, but then everything rushes rushes rushes

and I'm pushed back as the crowds try to high-five or wave or hold up their banners or just shout words of encouragement as the next player walks out. It's mayhem and the next thing I can recall is that Phil Taylor is on the stage handing some Canadian (do they even play?) his ass, and it's all getting a bit much so I work my way back to the relative safety of the media balcony and watch it all unfold from above.

A side note: as Phil walked down the tunnel accompanied by the other walk-on girl (blonde ying to the brunette's yang) a small boy was being held up, yelling and waving to catch Phil's attention, which he couldn't fail to do as I could hear the littler fucker screaming from up here. Phil walked over and touched the kid on the head in a very papal gesture. Like he was healing him. The kid's face transformed and lit up the whole of the civic hall. I scribbled a note: The Power is like the Pope.

As I'm waiting in the press room to meet The Power, I'm introduced to Russ 'The Voice' Bray, who is yet another person who is not only pleased to meet me but genuinely interested in the book that you are holding in your hands. And then a burly security guard leads a bigger man in a smart suit with an earpiece (who actually turns out to be the Aussie floor manager) who in turn leads The Power – who is short, grey and slightly tubby. Just how I like them – and who reminds me for some reason of a hamster. Turns out that he's got a train to catch but will go on the record for me for a few minutes. This is my first actual contact with a darting legend.

The Power is a straight-up northern bloke who also knows how to play the game. Magic Dave tells him about my book and The Power eyes me with suspicion. Looks like a London media type, he is thinking.

'Was it good to be mentored by Eric Bristow?' I ask.

'[laughing hard] Was it bollocks good. He made you a winner. You had to be a winner. He wouldn't sponsor you if you were a loser – you'd get a slap around the kisser. He'd tell you to fuck off. If you lost in the final

it would be, "Go fuck yourself, I don't want to talk to you." And you'd go and fuck yourself and practise harder, as he wouldn't want to know ...'

Barely a question or two in and it appears time is up. 'Will you sit down with me sometime soon?' I ask.

'Sure ...' The Power weebles out of the room and takes the bustle with him.

I wander down to the referees' room to shoot the breeze with Russ – who turns out to be an ex-cop, ex-scaffolder, and former darts player. We chat about whether darts is ever going to become an Olympic sport and Russ informs me that sat directly behind us is Steve Pegrum – one of the founder members of the PDC. I turn to say hello, but Steve is sitting in front of a large monitor playing some crazy fruit game on his mobile whilst acting as another referee. He is one of the few who put his life on the line to break away and form something new, something that wasn't the BDO.

Fat chewed, I wander out to catch the world's number one, Michael van Gerwen, make his grand entrance, only to find the third match well under way. This is my second real taste of the game live. I'm only a few feet away from sheer world-class greatness. I was nearly even closer when I took the wrong door that would have taken me directly onto the stage and out into the world via Sky Sports 1 HD. As van Gerwen hits a couple of 180s on the trot, the crowd (who are well on the way with the booze) sing that familiar and very catchy darts song, 'Da da da da ...' waving their 180 cards about with the backs turned to the camera to publicise their customisations. It's moments like this when the TV cameras are scanning the crowd for some crazy-assed and lairy reaction shots.

'I want Mr Sausage', 'Slug Nation', 'Thanks for the tickets, Chris', 'JFT 96', 'Arlewas Ladies Darts on Tour' and the timeless 'Sudgens Haulage'.

Watching Michael in the flesh pings me back to a couple of days before, when, for the first time ever, I was monitoring the live darts score online, hoping that the young German talent on the rise, Max Hopp, would stay in the competition until I got there on Wednesday. Mighty Mike brutally destroyed him in twelve minutes flat, and this was when it occurred to me that it takes well over the usual 10,000 hours to master this darting lark and then some. How the fuck do you keep getting better?

Back in the real, I witness something physically click within van Gerwen as he steps up to the oche with his giant foot sideways (all the players seem to be wearing the same strange black slip-on loafer-mutant shoes, a bit like the ones my son used to wear to school when he was twelve and his footwear needed to be bomb proof to even last a term) and shoots 137 leaving him 24 to make it 4 legs to 3. Then Robert Thornton mumbles up to score a paltry 60 and the look on his face tells me he knows that he has lost before the Dutch darts machine almost pushes him out of the way to finish the leg on 24 (12, double 6) and then steps it up another notch. MvG soon hits ten games and I scuttle up to the press room for my meet-and-greet.

But the world's best has other plans as Magic Dave tells me that he doesn't want to talk to me about darts in general as 'his head is in the game'. But I say hello and let him know that we need to be sitting down sometime soon.

Van Gerwen mutters something that sounds like 'just not tonight' before turning to joke with one of the PDC production team that he is 'looking very gay tonight', which is my cue to leave.

As I wander along the exit that will take me to the street I spot the walk-on girls doing Instagram shots with a long line of blushing (or just flushed) males. They seem happy to be doing this and I fight the urge to go and introduce myself as I know that there will be plenty of other opportunities and don't want to interrupt their work. Heaven can wait, I mutter. It's just then, as I turn to leave, that I'm approached by the third black guy in the building who introduces himself as Leon Davis. He's is keen to chat to me about my book and reveals that he is doing his Ph.D. thesis on the marketing of darts. This has just got interesting. This is why I drove however many hours from Barnet to Wolves to hang out with a bunch o' people that I wouldn't normally be hanging out with, nor they me. After chatting with Leon for a bit I walk out into the cold November night air and catch my breath.

My first impressions of the world of superstar Dartsland as I'm trying to get on the M6 to drive back to London: it is a fucking extra-terrestrial world, but one I can't help being fascinated by. It's so brutally honest about what it wants – money and darting fame for the players, and booze, 180s, more booze, and accessibility to the players and busty babes, for the fans. It's out there, and extreme in all senses of the word. As I motor on towards home, with the anthems of the evening rolling over in my mind, I feel satisfied at my first professional glimpse of this remarkable game.

CHAPTER FOUR

WINNERS AND LOSERS

'I keep getting asked to do my autobiography. A guy came up to me in Blackpool last year who'd done Torvill and Dean's ... and he said why hasn't someone done yours ... and I said I ain't gonna spend four, five months on something with no guarantee ...'

Keith Deller, ex-World Champion, failing to really grasp the definition of autobiography

The world that the old-school legends of darts slowly fade into after they retire from the grind of competitive darts is a strange, limbo-like place, where the beer is still cheap (often free), you can still smoke (as long as you crack open a window) and for one or two nights a week each month, you are still revered and worshipped as much as you were when you were the tabloid-fodder champion who regularly appeared on national TV egging the crowd on or winding up your opponent or just being well lairy. Almost. The back bone of this world are roads such as the A1 or the A13, which are legendary (and somewhat obsolete) themselves. Far from being glamorous, the cold harsh reality is that it's quite a hard slog for the legends to keep their names out there, but they have no other option. Dotted along these roads are venues such as the

Circus Tavern, Bar 501 in Bristol, and Gresham's Sports and Social Club, Ipswich, where, for the Legends of Darts night, a standard ticket is £20 and 'includes Beef-and-Guinness pie and chips'.

The 'legends exhibition' has become the bread and butter for any ex-champion. Get a couple of big names (Eric, Keith, Bobby, John …) stick them in a people-carrier with a fold-up oche and sound system in the back and schlep up and down the aforementioned roads charging up to £1,500 a night playing in clubs, pubs, dart associations, theme bars and soggy community centres packed to the rafters with a woozy crowd of swaying darts fans.

The punters get to spend some time up close and personal and sometimes even play their heroes. The players get paid. The booze flows and then there is often a Q & A at the end when the players spill the beans so we all find out the who, what, when, where, why.

I asked The Voice where the old legends go to die? The exhibition circuit?

'I've just done a Legends Night in a nightclub in Clapham, and the legends were Peter Manley (and he's only just about a legend), Bob Anderson, John Lowe, Keith Deller and Dennis Priestley,' Russ Bray told me, hanging about the players' warm-up area and half-price bar.

'And your favourite venue?' I asked.

'The Circus Tavern was a fabulous venue in its day but darts outgrew it. You couldn't get any more people in. The atmosphere – I tell you – in there was absolute electrical. You used to stand there and the crowd was four feet away and the players would walk back from the oche and they'd have people either side, literally right on top of them. Accessible – and that is what makes darts such a wonderful sport as well. Every person is accessible. Take your average idol in football or any other top sportsperson: you will never get to them. With your darts idol you can meet them on the street corner outside and he will sign the programme …' Russ Bray waxed lyrical, his love of darts shining through. But I'm not really buying it, not just yet. The world of the legends is set back in a time when men were men and women were always on their knees, but you will just have to hang about a bit more to see if this is true.

THE LEGEND OF LEGENDS

The raggedy-assed alien silhouette of a Scottish housing estate – or scheme – rising out of the damp dawn coastal fog greets me as I crunch in between the dark buildings that loom above like the two statues at the gates of Valhalla. I am deep in the land of legends; way out of my comfort zone. I am beyond north in the heart of Scotland in a place they used to call Lang Toun – but today is known locally as Chinatown – although on the map it says Kirkcaldy – to pay my respects to the legend they once called Gumsy and to show that I'm not just some hipster twat slumming it for book material.

This story began the day before, when I was stood outside the trendy Edinburgh café Valvona and Crolla, thinking hard about the fact that nobody knows nothing. If I were some moody literary-type who gave two shits about proper grammar, I'd probably say that nobody knows anything, but I'm not and this isn't that kind of story; it's not even that kind of book. I also want to fuck with the rules a bit as I know there are no rules, demonstrated by this here story. Which is about how a darting star – with the greatest rags-to-riches-to-rags story of all time – can be born out of the most impossible hardships and such a miserable existence, then cross over from the fringes of society in a Scottish council estate into mainstream 'it's him off the TV' land and nobody will see him/it coming; nobody apart from the man himself will have absolute faith in what is going to happen, and then absolutely no faith at all, and nobody will call it until it's all over and done with.

Which was a bit like when Irvine Welsh delivered the manuscript of *Trainspotting* to his publishers in 1992. At best they hoped it would become one of those edgy underground cult classics that a handful of people (the so-called early-adopters in horrible adman adspeak) read and then mutter about amongst themselves, which then might have a knock-on cultural effect in some other mediums – music or film, perhaps – but never the written word, as that's the realm of proper writers, ones who have had a proper Oxbridge education. But ye olde gods of Buckfast were watching and made sure every-fucker tuned into the book; we all got wrapped up with the alternative zeitgeist it offered. Back then nobody was writing about the fact that the youth were taking a shitload of drugs, unless they were trust-fund kids into William Burroughs and the like, which was just boring and so predictable, and Hunter had stopped writing properly a decade or so before. The publisher may have seen something twinkling in those dark pages that was of literary interest. Perhaps they hoped that the cultural content spoke directly to tons of people in the country – that it actually said something about the lives they were leading. Their punt was rewarded.

And as I was in Scotland I thought I'd better check in with Irvine to see if he could shed some cultural light on my mission, on the cultural role today of the Scottish scheme, the part of Jocky Wilson, and his thoughts on the game itself.

'Not only can you play it in a pub, you usually play better after a couple of drinks. You are better if you are a solid squat fat bastard – your frame grounds you as you chuck the dart. It's a "sport" for the unfit,' Irvine reckoned, as we walked downhill towards his beloved Leith.

'And what about the role of street culture in your work?' I had to ask.

'Street culture hasn't influenced my work, more like it's the totality of it. Just with the changes we had in the last twenty years it's harder to find unmodified street culture that isn't media culture, that hasn't been subsumed into the media; and that's why I'm somewhat stuck in an eighties time-warp when I do my writing.'

Irvine has always been fascinated by that era of transition when we changed from one thing into another. Back then you could have a vibrant street culture that wasn't instantly sucked into the media, used for some commercial reason and then regurgitated. To some extent there is still some original culture in Edinburgh – in some of the estates like Burdiehouse.

'I'm way too old to be able to get in there now. You have to be fourteen to find your way into that; as soon as you're old enough to publish books or shoot films you are part of the media, whether you like it or not. I just know that these little fuckers are having a great time and doing some wonderful things,' he told me as we tried to find something original still standing. Something from way back when.

The Scottish housing schemes were created after the streets – where Irvine Welsh grew up – had fallen into disrepair and parts were scheduled for slum clearance. Schemes like Muirhouse. Which leads me the next day to the place Jocky began and ended his days on earth – a Scottish scheme half an hour's drive to the north-east of Edinburgh.

'Jocky was a quintessential Scot, a wee guy with a chip on his shoulder who took on the British establishment.' Irvine sealed the deal. 'He even married an Argentinian during the Falklands War …' The original darting rebel.

> *He's sixteen stone of fat and pain*
> *When he steps up the oche*
> *When he throws the spears you can hear the cheers*
> *For Fife's wee hero Jocky.*

When he was ten, Jocky's wayward dad Willie was sent down for fencing, and I don't mean the spindly swordsman sport, and the effect of this was that his mother couldn't keep the home together on her own and work several jobs to make ends meet. It all began to fall apart so Jocky and his younger brother Tommy spent five years living at the St Margaret's House orphanage, a few miles north of Kirkcaldy, his hometown. Jocky had always been unwilling to talk about the beginning of his life as it was so hard, but then again so was the end. Jocky was born John Thomas Wilson in Kirkcaldy, Fife, on 22 March

1950, but after his rise to fame was known as Gumsy due to the lack of any teeth.

'People might think that having no teeth snookers you when it comes to eating,' Wilson remembered in his 1983 autobiography, *Jocky*. 'But I can manage just about anything with my gums. I can chew a steak provided it's well done. I can even eat apples. Great Yarmouth rock and nuts are the only two things that defeat me.'

After the usual travesty of no one giving a fuck about him at school, followed by a two-year spell in the army, Jocky tried his hand as a spud peeler, fish guts remover, back-breaking labourer in a paint powder factory, deep-seam miner, and coal delivery man. A litany of miserable, cold, hard jobs in the pissing Scottish rain. Enough to lead a man to drink and smoke and lose his teeth.

By nineteen, he liked to spend the majority of his free time hanging out in the Lister Bar (now a low-end supermarket), which according to Jocky had 'a wee bit of the hustler atmosphere that Minnesota Fats and Paul Newman would have appreciated', and was not that far from his council flat, and it was in this bar one fateful day that he was asked to play for the darts team. This ended badly after he was completely humiliated by his opponent, who was on the last double before Jocky got off his first – a position I've been in myself recently and it sucks big time. I was almost in tears, but Jocky went home and put up a dartboard and began to practise. Day and night. Night and day. Thunk. Thunk. Thunk.

But the tubby wee man rapidly found that he had a rare talent for darts and was soon out with his homeboy 'Super-Spar Willie', hustling the pubs and clubs of Kirkcaldy to earn some extra cash for beer and fags and sweets. Jocky had few more vices than the sweets that took all his teeth by the time he was twenty-eight.

Within a very short space of time he was playing for the most excellent Fife team and thanks to his prestigious talent with the arrows, almost unbelievably, was soon the captain of the Scottish darts team. It was in this role that he began to beat the English stars, which is always good to boost the morale of the Scottish, and by now he had discovered the finer tipple of 'Magic Coke' (half a bottle of coke mixed with the cheapest, most industrial vodka), which probably marked the beginnings of his descent into darting hell.

'You could always rely on him,' said Jimmy Skirving, one of Jocky's many drinking partners from the Lister Bar. 'But I can assure you Jocky was taken advantage of. Once he won a holiday and some suitcases. He got home with neither – he sold the holiday for fifty quid and the cases for a tenner.'

Jocky was still on the dole by 1978 but somehow got enough cash together to enter the Butlin's Grand Masters, in Ayrshire, where he came second and won £500 in the form of one of those giant cheques, which he would proudly carry aloft to show all and sundry around the bars of Kirkcaldy. One of the paper-pushing jobs-worths at his local social services either saw this in person or watched his win on TV, and not long after Jocky's dole stopped abruptly.

By the end of the year he was already in the world's top ten players, and rising swiftly through the rankings until he won his first World Championship title on 16 January 1982 (the year he also won the British Open Championship). It was at this time that darts was reaching its first zenith. He beat the number two seed – John 'Stoneface' Lowe – 5–3.

'I sunk double 16 to win, and I was champ. I was drained of effort and just about in tears,' Wilson recalled.

As we've already heard, Jocky and Eric Bristow had one of the greatest rivalries ever seen (and probably won't ever be surpassed) in the game of darts. Scotland vs. England. The Huns vs. the FEBs (fucking English bastards). The toothless underdog vs. the crafty cockney. After Alan Evans, Bristow was the second superstar of darts, and by the early eighties he was a bona fide sporting celebrity, with a soft spot for digging out darts players north of the border, which was all great backstory to build and hype the clash of clashes. The 1989 World Championship (some seven years after Jocky's first world title win) had a divided nation on the edge of their seats. Eric Bristow might have been the more skilful player, but everyone was rooting for the underdog Jocky.

But left to his own devices, it may have never happened for Jocky. Along the way he was mentored by Bobby George, who also made the pilgrimage to Jocky's council flat, decades before me.

'It was like Fagin's kitchen, drunken people, bottles everywhere, chucking wood on the fire – it could have been the furniture.' Bobby George recalled in *Bellies and Bullseyes*, and vowed to help Jocky become a proper darts player after witnessing such carnage.

Back to Eric vs. Jocky. The game itself was an epic tale of how – after storming through to a 5–0 lead with Eric looking simply stunned beneath his badly applied highlights – Jocky seemed to lose his bottle and Bristow mounted a killer comeback to tie the game at 5–5. Both players were within a dart of finishing, but it was Jocky who won the match with a double 10, after which he sank to his knees, and kissed Eric's hand, which was probably the most tender and genuine moment in all of darting folklore, considering the undisputed rivalry between the two players.

And that was Jocky's moment on live TV, watched by millions around the world and probably by everybody in Scotland, for this was much much more than a darts match at Lakeside. This was revenge on the English for a lifetime of bastardness, and if a small fat toothless man from a scheme in Fife could do it, so could anybody, and the fact that it had taken Jocky a long time to win his second world title made it worth so much more, framing him as a shining light of hope, albeit one that was slowly extinguished with booze. After this victory, Jocky toured the land and the world thanks to his darting achievements, and I know he had a blinding time.

The craziness gradually began to catch up with him when he suffered a series of health problems, and was offered a choice: give up the fags and booze or die. He chose the former and that was the end of the darts. Jocky couldn't play without drinking. He tried for a while, but like a Jazz musician without the dope, the magic just wasn't there.

'My illnesses meant I had no energy. And I could not be Jocky Wilson on a dartboard without the drink. So I packed it in and came home. I have no regrets.'

By 1996 Jocky – aged only forty-five – had stopped going out in public and was resigned to being 'all washed up and finished with darts'. The first-ever Scottish World Champion had long since stopped throwing the arrows, and suffered from arthritis, diabetes and depression. He refused all interview requests after his last public appearance in 1995 at the same Butlin's holiday camp in Ayr where his darting adventure had begun. His daily commute was from bed to TV and back again. I've got tears in my eyes typing these words because this story is soaked in such inevitability; such hope, promise, talent and opportunity snuffed out ruthlessly by a more powerful hopelessness, carried downstream in the river of booze.

'I still watch the lads on Sky. And I swear like fuck at the twats that used to wind me up. Eric. Lowey. The ones I used to stuff,' he told Sid Waddell, the last and only person to get an audience with Jocky in the years leading up to his death.

It's while I'm writing this story on Jocky that I realise how far darts has travelled and how alien it was to me. I was just a visitor; a day-tripping hipster, indeed. I'm not worthy.

Back in the housing estate I know that there will be no blue plaque, no lasting memorial or any kind of recognition that this was the place of birth and death of the first Scottish hero of darts, but I pay my respects, walk away, and dry my eyes.

Jocky has to have the last word: 'I've been let down once or twice in my life, but I don't want anyone feeling sorry for me. There's only one person to blame for the situation I'm in, and that's me.'

THE POWER

'I have been in Japan, China, Australasia and Australia and New Zealand with Phil Taylor who I often go for a walk with in the morning and everyone – from old to new – is coming up to him saying, "Hello, Phil!" Now you're looking at a guy who's dominated the industry for twenty-five years and won sixteen world titles, over two hundred titles worldwide and there isn't a TV channel he hasn't been on one way or another.'

John McDonald, fearless MC

As you've already heard, the first proper legend I met – at Wolverhampton Civic Hall – was Phil Taylor, who had just begun winding down his record-breaking career and working less as he was feeling the strain from thirty years of solid darts. I watch him play several times but we don't meet again until a few months later – at the Circus Tavern, where he is headlining in the Masters of Darts exhibition match against The Bronzed Adonis, Steve Beaton. Over this space of time I had tried to get into the mind of a darting legend, but I think I just wound him up with my elementary questions. 'Read my book!' he keeps saying, after I ask him something he must have presumed I would know.

'Has it not all become a grind?'

'I want to enjoy it all now because I'm slowing down. The schedule's busier and I find the travelling harder, but this has been my life for over twenty-five years. I'm looking to relax and enjoy my life since I'm coming towards the end of my career. I'll still play in the events I've qualified for and that I'm invited to, but away from that I'm slowing down now.'

Phil – born and bred in Stoke-on-Trent – is the greatest darts player ever and is not known to suffer fools, which ensured I had my work cut out. His hair is grey and sparse, and he comes across as a straight-up northern working-class sort of guy. A 'don't fuck with me and you'll be okay' kind of man. And my next question winds him up, when I ask if the players of today who haven't come out of the pub are any different.

'I came out of pub culture, the youngsters haven't. They haven't got the respect, that's the trouble. They haven't had a clip round the ear hole – when I was a youngster you use your lip in the pub it was either put them up or shut that up – no two ways about it. You use your lip you get a smack around the kisser, you want me to be honest, I will be honest with you.'

'So they are looked after, then?'

'They are in an environment where people like Dave Allen/the PDC protect them. You can't touch them. So they come in all cocky, all cocksure, and you can't do nothing about it. But it will happen. It will happen. I wanna play a game in the final. I want to slap them to death.'

'When you started winning, did Eric Bristow really let you know how much you still owed him?'

'Every fucking day!'

'And how are you feeling about playing these days?'

'I'm feeling alright, and for me now it's about rest and practice, and that's what I'll be doing. I've got to get my preparation right but I've played well this year. It is all about preparation and that's what I'm targeting.'

At the start of 2017, Phil announced that it would be his last year of darts. That he was retiring.

'I'm just going to enjoy each match. If I get beat, I get beat. If I don't, I don't. Whatever happens it's going to be the last one. Unless you pay me a lot more money. At the end of the year, that is me done. Done,' he says with a rather poetic finality.

'What is it like being a legend?' is what I really wanted to know.

'I haven't got time to sit back and think about it. Monday I'm in a school in Macclesfield, Tuesday, Wednesday and Thursday I'm in Newcastle. Friday I'm in Cumbria. This is what your life's like – you are literally on the road more or less seven days a week. It's not easy, trust me, not when you're getting on for sixty years old. It's hard when you're playing against youngsters who can do four or five hours of practice. I used to do that – can't do it any more.'

'But will you miss it?' I want to know.

'I won't miss it. I've had that buzz for thirty years so I think the buzz is now past me, but I will always be involved with darts. If Sky wanted me then we will talk and if they don't it doesn't matter. I'll do me exhibitions, I'll do me personal appearances ...'

Pulling away for a second here, I had realised I needed to get another perspective on what is now a fading legend, so I had turned to Gary Anderson, who is the world's number two, to see what he thought about Phil.

'Taylor had everyone in his pocket for years but the problem Michael [van Gerwen] has got now is there's so many young players coming through that he might only be able to dominate for a few years,' Gary told me.

'But what about the next wave of challengers?'

'There's always someone who comes up through the ranks to take a game to a new level. Just look at snooker with Steve Davis, Stephen Hendry and then Ronnie O'Sullivan. So that's why I don't think Michael will be able to emulate what Phil Taylor has done in years to come.' Gary puts his money where his mouth is, with regards to the chance of Michael van Gerwen ever equalling Phil's record.

Phil Taylor has been the undisputed superstar of darts ever since winning his first title (the Canadian Open) in 1988. In 1990 he made it to the final of the Winmau World Masters as a 125–1 outsider, up against his mentor – now his rival – Eric Bristow. Phil took the title 6–1 and went on to dominate darts for the next twenty-seven years, winning a total of 216 professional tournaments, 84 major titles and 16 world championships. An indelible stain on his record was that in 1999 Taylor was found guilty of "indecently groping" two female darts fans in the back of his campervan in Scotland; he was fined £2,000 and had his MBE nomination rescinded. He maintained in a *Guardian* interview in 2003 that he was the victim of a tabloid sting. I am planning on catching up with Phil later ...

KEITH

The A12 as I drive towards Ipswich is peppered with sex shops next to fifties-style diners and truck stops. It's a cold, miserable, dark and drizzly Saturday afternoon in February and I'm heading up to watch Keith Deller and Kevin Painter take on all-comers in aid of Ipswich Town FC Academy Association.

I first met Keith Deller at his stand, slap bang in the middle of the Fans' Village at the World's, where you could have your photo taken with a darting legend for twenty quid. Oversized credit card logos suggested that cash is not the only accepted payment, and the other names on offer were Peter Manley, John Part and Rod Harrington. One afternoon, Russ Bray introduced me to someone who turned out to be the 'comeback kid' himself, Keith Deller, who on a little investigating turned out to be the original Keith in darts and the inspiration for Martin Amis's Keith Talent.

'On its tiny scale it's elemental with a thrilling milieu. It's really a sort of tiddlywinks in a bear pit,' reckoned Martin Amis, talking about darts in the BBC film *Bullseyes and Beer: When Darts Hit Britain*. And he would know – he must have done a fair bit of research for his novel *London Fields*: surely the greatest ever novel set in the world of darts and one of the best London-based novels of all time. Written in the early eighties, the book's anti-hero is Keith Talent, a lower-than-low petty criminal, supreme cheat, a lying thieving whoring fool, but above all, an absolute darts fanatic and wannabee champion. The book is rich and sharp and practically re-invented the form of the novel, but the key narrative that sucked me in was Keith's rise to the semi-finals of the Duoshare Sparrows Masters. The book was published in 1988, and would have been a vital moment for darts. Up till then no one in the literary world (readers, writers, critics, teachers) would have given darts a second thought since darts was swiftly heading for the wilderness. But the book – 'Darts innit' is one of Keith's many catchphrases – introduced the game to a whole new demographic, who would in turn go on to talk, write and spread the word about the cultural phenomenon of darts.

As part of his research, Martin Amis hung out with darting legend Keith Deller, who in 1983, as a 23-year-old complete outsider/ qualifier from Ipswich, beat the world's top three players, including Eric Bristow in a memorable final. It was one of the greatest upsets in the sport's history.

I hung out with the real Keith that afternoon and we got talking about *London Fields*. 'I met Martin in a wine bar in Enfield,' Keith recalled, thinking back to the mid-eighties. 'He walked in and asked me what I'd like to drink and I ordered a sparkling water. He had a pint of lager and in them days you could smoke in the restaurants, and he had a roll-up and he said, "I can't work this one out – there you are slim and drinking a mineral water and here's me with a fag on – that's the wrong way round." And the next minute … *London Fields*. Keith [Talent] was the World Champion, the wife was Kim, which is my wife's name. He really based it on the interview that I was doing.'

'Did you read the book?' I had to ask.

'No. I haven't read it …' and Keith didn't see the irony in this. I'm saying nothing, except imagine knowing there was a book out there and the central character was based on you …

The bottom line was that the real Keith had been able to stage such a darting upset because he was a clean-living, non-smoking, next-generation of players. The literary Keith, on the other hand, was just in it for the birds and the fame and the booze and the TV. The deep and meaningfuls.

'It's the drastic elevation into darts superstardom that made Keith come alive for me. And he says, "I can handle it. Fame, I can handle it …"' Martin remembers what made Keith Talent so special in *Bullseyes and Beer: When Darts Hit Britain*. 'I watched a great deal of it on TV and we're talking about an era – the early eighties – where you know it was a very mercurial atmosphere at these events …'

I asked Keith if it would be possible to come from nowhere today and win the World's as an absolute outsider, as he had done in '83.

'I don't think it would. I won two, three tournaments in America and they asked me to play in the Los Angeles Open, which I did and won that, then I went to the play-offs in London, and won that – easy. Got a play-off for the World Championship, and went on to win it. I told the presenter that I'd win at the beginning of the week because I thought I would. I'd already beaten Eric two or three times. I'd beaten John Lowe, I'd beaten Bob Anderson, so I'd beat a few of them ...'

'So you knew you were going to win?'

'[Iconic *Blue Peter* presenter] Peter Purves asked me how I would do and I said that I would be World Champion as no one would stop me. I honestly believed it. When I won the Los Angeles Open they were all in it and I won it well. None of them would want to play me at Jollees ... It was an old nightclub but it had a good atmosphere. It was great, I liked it on top of you ...'

And there you have another golden darting insight: even though the venue was a complete shit hole and the punters were breathing down your neck, this only enhanced the atmosphere, and added to the momentum. Add to this the fact that deep down in your mind you knew that you were going to win – you were on a roll and each win just increased your confidence – and you produce the biggest upset in darting history. Keith Deller not only beat Eric Bristow to win the 1983 World Championship, he beat John Lowe in the quarter-final and Jocky Wilson in the semi. And this led me to ask about the darting culture – or basically getting well pissed and then playing better, which as we've seen with Jocky, worked for a while.

'Ours was a very old-school lifestyle back in those days; you had a beer or a pint but we were still professionals. I didn't drink a lot. I didn't smoke, so I was different compared to Eric and Jocky and Bobby who all used to smoke. I had a more clean-cut image ...' Keith said.

WOLFIE

When I was working on this book I spent some time researching the BDO, and I'll be honest, I had real trouble giving a flying fuck about the players who weren't women. The men all merged into one and this may seem a bit harsh, but as far as I could tell if you want to check out a geezer playing quality darts, then you head straight to the PDC. It's no secret. Then, the day after my complete savaging on the dimly lit oche by the Filipino in New Barnet, I met Martin 'Wolfie' Adams and for a short while and I changed my mind.

Wolfie Adams is one of the figureheads of the modern-day BDO, and he's the perfect man for the job. He is a walking manifestation of the BDO: solid. Three times World Champion. Likes a drink and a smoke. Proudly rocks some well-lairy tomfoolery. Fans love him so he hangs around the Lakeside foyer and will gladly let you get a photo if you put something into the collection jar of the BDO's charity of choice, usually children's cancer. He's the sort of person who keeps his Superkings in one of those purse-like containers. Huge belly. Laughs a lot. A really decent bloke. I mean that. I'm not taking the piss.

Martin has been around the block, thrice times, and has been part of the BDO since 1992. Unusually he didn't start playing darts until his thirties, after being made redundant by Lloyds Bank. He turned professional aged thirty-six. Thanks to the formation of the PDC and their players' subsequent ban from county and national darts, a gap opened up that enabled Martin to become the longest-serving England darts captain ever. He got the moniker 'Wolfie' after he drunkenly heckled a DJ and was told to comb his moody wolf-like beard, and there was me thinking it was some obscure power-to-the-people Citizen Smith reference.

Unlike me, Wolfie discovered he could actually throw a dart by accident after his cousin set up a board in his garage and the two of them would have a muck-about and a beer. Turns out one of them was really good. 'He asked me over and I beat him on his own board,'

Martin told me, sipping his pint. And with my darting travesty still fresh in my mind, I'm keen to explore the link between booze and darts. Do you play better when you've had a drink?

'You think you do. It's a habit. Drinking within the sport of darts is just something we do. Sometimes the players have too much and then their game goes right off, but if you feel right, then you'll play well.'

'But the media have been using booze as a club to beat darts with since that *Not the Nine O'Clock News* sketch, haven't they?' I asked.

'For whatever reason, journalistically, people don't like the fact that we like a drink. We've always liked a drink. Footballers try and hide it in a nightclub – which is a damn silly place to try and hide a drink. The golfers in the nineteenth hole. The rugby players are pretty open about it because they've got their rugby club. The darts players just do it in any old pub they can find. We're no different to so many other sports. They all claim they don't drink, but they do. They slaughtered Wayne Rooney for just having a glass of bubbly at a wedding. That's madness.

'The pub is the atmosphere and area that we've grown up in. We don't smoke in or around where we are playing because we are not allowed to any more. The law says that. We stopped drinking and smoking on stage in 1988, well before the smoking ban came in. There was no smoking or drinking on TV,' Martin told me as he finished his drink.

'Did that affect the game?' I asked, nodding to the barman for another round. I was trying to obliterate my memories of the previous day.

'No. Well, it affected one or two of the old guard. Jocky Wilson took to eating wine gums. I'm not sure which was best – him eating a wine gum or smoking a fag! You've got to err on the side of the wine gums. That's the way Jocky handled it.'

'It's the sport you can't clean up.' I dropped one of my darting mantras.

'I don't think you can regulate drinking and smoking out of any sport. It's part of our history, you know. It might not be the part of the history that you are proud of …'

'A bit like the jocularity between players?' Martin raises his eyebrows at my use of that word.

'One of the things that's missing in the PDC is the banter amongst players. There is none, basically. You won't see a practice room like we have here, over there. They have even got two halves of the practice room now because there are players that don't get on with each other; so they can practise in separate halves of the room. There is a screen down the middle so they can't even see each other. It's probably the most boring environment in the world, for darts.'

Seeing as talk had turned to the PDC I have to ask, 'Why are you so loyal to the BDO?'

'It was the BDO that gave me the opportunities to become the player that I am. Not just the BDO board, but all the volunteer officials in every county and super league. It's not in my nature to turn my back on all the help and support I've received from those people over the last twenty years or so. Loyalty seems to be a dirty word in some quarters these days. Far too many people want to take out and never put something back.'

Interlude #4 – Arrows with Uncle Joe

'You have to learn how to lose before you can learn how to win …'
Martin 'Wolfie' Adams inadvertently channelling
Kareem Abdul-Jabbar, with the kind of advice
I really need to start listening to …

To say my first officially sanctioned game of darts was a complete disaster would be a lie. It was a dream that turned swiftly into a fucking nightmare, and to this day I can't really believe what went down. In this case I'm hoping that fiction is stranger than truth, and either way, you'll just have to ride this one out as I give you a rather condensed recap, for obvious reasons, and brush this shit firmly under the carpet.

The location is a sports and social club minutes away from the original office of the BDO in North London, the kind of place that allows you to vape at the bar and the drink is almost as cheap as the student union its patrons never went to. The brightest parts of the interior would be the row of dartboards to the left of the main bar, if the little lights above the board are switched on. The walls are lined with framed posters for darting events and West End musicals, which is an interesting combination. To the right there is a function room subtly separated off with one of those sun-bleached yellow vinyl concertina doors. Naturally the magnet has broken and so it won't close properly. When I stick my nose through it looks like a car boot sale after an earthquake, with tat everywhere that someone just couldn't bring themselves to throw out. I spot a faded yellow straw dartboard surround sponsored by a brewery that went out of business decades ago, which would have once proudly framed the board during an official match or exhibition.

I'm early and so go to the bar and order a pint of shandy to elevate me from the bleakness. The only people who are here are the heavyweight North London all-day drinkers; establishments like this revolve around such patronage like alcohol-fuelled satellites. I drink it quickly and eat some salt and vinegar crisps. I order another pint and ask the guy behind the bar to turn on the lights by the dartboards as that is why I'm here: to take on their number-one player, Joe.

The sarky barman laughs and says something about Stalin, which goes over my head and then mutters something about fucking tourists as he has to walk three feet to the till, behind which the light switches sit. He flicks them on and the place erupts in protest.

'Turn that off!' is the general consensus, as the dark alcoholic shadow is what they are buying into in this place, that and the very reasonable prices. The barman scoffs and whacks off the two nearest lights leaving on the furthest, weakest, most pathetic yellow bulb, which appeases the baying crowd.

Who by now are checking out this fucking interloper who has wandered into their somnolent world. It's at this point I realise that I should buy them all a drink . . .

After a few more shandies, the guy I'm meant to be playing rattles up and it turns out he isn't really called Joe. That's his nickname – Joe Stalin – as it's said that he used to be a bit of a communist. Everyone draped over the bar heckles him and I think I may even join in as I'm a bit pissed by now. You can see where this is heading.

'Joe' is handed a J2O and heads straight for the oche. I chug my drink and go to the toilet, which is the highlight of this sad story. It all goes downhill from here . . .

Joe lets me warm up for ten minutes. He nods hello but that is all. No words. He leans back drinking his juice, observing me as I miss the board, drop my arrows, lose the flights, hit the wall, have another piss, hit the bar, hammer a triple-20 home only for it to ping out and I have to jump out of the way, knocking Joe into the wall and spilling what remains of his juice. Went well, then.

I am desperately trying to put something back into the game but I don't even get off 501 because we're playing double in double out and there is no way around it. I am drunk and I am shite. Joe goes in on double top and out on a double 15, turns to me and looks right through me, as if to say, There is no point in this – you're not even here, which means you're not even good practice. He packs up his darts, places his bottle back on the bar and walks away without a word to anyone.

The barman flicks off the lights and after a moment standing alone in the dark to get my shit together I stumble out into the dusk. I've been here before, just not as tragic as this.

CHAPTER FIVE

THE FANS

'When I first saw darts on TV I was like, Why is that on Sky Sports? And then I started watching it and got into it. I was hooked straight away, within like ten minutes.'

Alice, eighteen-year-old darts fan

I was having a chat with Jelle Klaasen just outside the World's press office when I first met Dave and Kim, a straight-up River Island (they shun Stone Island round here) couple from Leigh-on-Sea, who were hanging about the hospitality entrance looking a bit lost. So I did my Good Samaritan act and wandered over to make sure they were okay.

'Just waiting for our mate who's got the tickets,' Dave told me. 'Trying to keep warm!'

'Sweet,' came my standard reply. 'Just making sure you're not lost ...'

'Thanks ...' he said, and as I was walking away his girlfriend whispered something to him and I instinctively turned back.

'Is there any chance you could get us a photo with Jelle ...?' Dave asked hopefully. They were so polite and nice I couldn't help being Freddie Fixer for a moment, so I bowled over and put in their request.

Jelle laughed of course and came over and I took the photo of the three of them just as Dave and Kim's squad of mates walked in on a glorious scene. It took a beat for them to spot what was happening before they shouted their approval. Jelle and I walked away, back to his manager, who was in the process of arranging some access for me with the rising Dutch star in the hood, which never actually came about.

It's from moments like this that darting friendships are born.

My first experience embedded with fans occurs on the second night of the World's with a gang of Swiss boys who are all dressed like Andre Agassi: huge blond highlighted wigs (Black Lace crossed with George Michael), black eighties tracksuits with red and turquoise detailing, golden Elvis sunglasses and topped off with big-assed dangling medallions.

'We are a football team from Switzerland,' a ginger moustache (stick-on) told me after I sat down at their table. 'There are many of us all around—' He pointed across the arena, where I could see a couple more of the Agassi clones sat high up in the bleachers, next to the TV studio room, their wigs standing out a mile.

'How long are you here for?'

'Just two days. We have to be back at work on Monday ...' It was at this point that a dark brooding unshaven hunk dressed in a small red dress with his balls almost hanging out the bottom walked up and started yak-yakking to us in what sounded like German, before abruptly jogging off.

'Who the fuck was that?' I asked.

'He is in the first football team in our town. We are the third. That is why he was dressed like an idiot.'

'What do you mean?'

'The first team take it too seriously. We don't care, hence why we are drunk and dressed like this and they are just prancing about like our bitches.'

'But, which darts players are you into?'

'Anderson. Wright.'

'What about van Gerwen?' I prodded, which resulted in a stream of German–Swiss that I couldn't understand but got the gist of. The jug of beer got passed and someone scored 180 or something on the stage and everyone was on their feet and that song started again and we were all singing and spilling beer and shouting shit in German–Swiss (me in Cape slang) at and about the first team who can suck our collective dicks. We are the Agassi Dart Boys and we don't fear. Drink your women and shag your beer. Or something like that.

I got a couple of jugs in and this was when I discovered the Ally Pally shuffle: two jugs. Eight pints. Motion. Keep one from slopping then the other. It's a bit like patting your head and rubbing your stomach but with booze involved. Easy when you know how; with a beer buzz topping it off it's fucking near on impossible. Fuck me, I was all over the shop.

Back at the table, the drinks lasted about a minute and then another Andre was off to cash in his sixteen tokens for another couple of jugs of shitty burpy lager.

By now I've seen how much alcohol plays a role in the darting world. It's a huge element both front of house and behind the scenes, but I have to go on the record saying that none of the PDC officials or workers ever drink whilst they are working. They need to keep a clear head to keep the machine oiled. I, on the other hand, often got a bollocking from one of the security guards for walking into the press pit drinking a pint whilst wearing my press pass. At moments like these all I had to do was to look around at the thousands of men chugging jugs and singing and chanting and getting rowdier by the minute and chug my pint down so the bloke would move the security barrier and let me pass.

I bided my chums farewell and followed a trio of Donald Trumps who soon were freaking me out a little – my head was struggling to maintain its grasp on reality. I stopped them for a photo and this was one of the images that will haunt me for quite some time. All three held jugs of beer and one of the masks sported a ripped mouth like a fish caught on a barb by an angler and it was such an eerie sight.

A bit later on that same night I saw my first bit of trouble. A young stacked drunk lad in a white V-neck jumper, no shirt, was being led out of the main arena by a number of security guards. As I'd been walking around the arena I'd noticed how many guys in black suits with striped ties (first seen in Wolverhampton) were stood around with their backs to the game, watching the fans like hawks on steroids. It's like they were expecting trouble.

The French or Belgian bouncer laughed when I asked him if they got much trouble. 'Every night. The later the competition the more trouble. The more drinking the more trouble.'

'I've only seen one guy getting walked out.'

'Stick around and you will be lucky. You will see fist fights. The other night we had to eject a whole gang of men in Lycra who kept jumping on the table with it all hanging out. They didn't want to go, of course.'

I mentioned that it's £120 a ticket from the touts.

'It's only 180 in there ...' He nodded back to the VIP seating area with table service, which is where I was headed to find Dave and Kim.

Everything – from the food to the gambling to the drink to the merch – is part of a revenue stream that flows directly back to the coffers of the PDC, aka Matchroom Sport Ltd, to give it its official name. The tickets are reasonably priced for a reason – they are just the start of the cash cow that gets slaughtered every night, along with the rest of us.

'Barry understands the audience and what he can attract. And he understands that he can attract a range of classes by keeping it relatively cheap. Keeping it where you still need a disposable amount of income but it's only a short-term commitment. But with any post-modern/liquid modern sport (the end of the '80s early '90s) you have to appeal to all classes. All different consumers.

Customers,' Leon Davis told me as we navigated our way through the carnage of the VIP area.

Before I know it I'm sat with Dave and Kim at their table and I'm getting as wasted as the rest of the place and suddenly the magic of darts takes over.

The ritual goes like this: Drink. Sing. Drink. Stand up and sing about how the other seats are shit. Sit down and drink. Jump about, mugging for the TV cameras. Drink. The whole place stands up when someone scores 180. Go to the toilet. Drink some more. Sing. Stand, and sometimes keep your eye on the state of the game happening some distance away on the stage, where – if you look over – the dartboard is the size of a five-pence piece.

'I've been twice already this year,' Kim told me. 'And I wanted Dave to see why it was so good.'

'Usually the other way round,' I presumed in response. Kim gave me a look as if to say, Not this time. None of your sexist presumption.

'I love it,' Dave reckoned. 'My dad was always on about it and has been going all his life but I never thought it would be like this!'

'Like what?'

'It's people like us on a night out that isn't just the normal bar, curry, club, back to mine ... It's different.'

'In what way?' I probed but Dave couldn't be bothered to think too deep and his train of thought wandered off with a gang of passing bishops.

'It's like a mad ritual,' Kim explained, 'where they get all dressed up and that and then get really fucked.'

'A very British one at that!' I added.

'Yeah. We like a tear-up at least once a month.' Dave's interest has been piqued by the topic of having it. I don't know if Dave is talking about the two or them or the British in general.

'You seen any drugs yet?' I asked a bit keenly.

'No.' And I could tell they are not sure if I'm asking cos I want some or just being a nosy writer (the truth was a bit of both).

'How thorough was your search?' I pressed my line of enquiry – as I've spent a fair bit of time watching the security searching people.

'Mine was a bit close … if you know what I mean.' Dave nodded down there.

'She said my eyeliner was a bit sharp,' Kim said.

'What – you were trying to bring a shank in?' I joked.

The truth of the matter was that I hadn't once been searched as the bouncers always saw the word media on my pass, even though every day I came in I had the previous day's press pass on and no one cared. At first it was strange to see a Teletubby getting a thorough pat-down but by now I'm pretty blasé … The VIPs seemed to get a much more thorough search than the regular fans.

Then then then the three of us are walking down the steep hill towards the station and I'm pretty wasted as I'm such a lightweight. I've only drunk a few shandies so I'm not spinning or any such shit, and the conversation and freezing December air is keeping me from tipping over into the abyss. It's safe to say that we're all a bit chatty and it's halfway through this journey that it occurs to me that I don't even know who won the darts. All I can remember is the place erupting in the biggest roar, we all jumped up and sang and danced to the 'Da da da da …' song and then we were all walking out into the freezing December night.

'Who the fuck won tonight?' I ask.

'Jelle got beat …' Kim tells me, a bit gutted.

'Shit, I wanted to interview him and now he's fucked off back to …' I'm not sure where it is, but I know he won't be hanging around.

'That security guard was so in love with you,' Dave remembers, which draws a bit of a blank from me.

'What was I doing?'

'He kept telling us that you couldn't be sat there in the VIP with your media pass consuming as you were. He wanted you to go and stand in the media pen at the bottom of the stage.'

'Sounds about right for me.'

'You spent ages explaining what it meant to be a gonzo writer ... and how you had to be sat with us!' Kim rolls her eyes at the memory. 'I think he wished he'd kept his mouth shut.'

'Soz. I never said I wasn't a twat,' I apologise.

'One of the defining elements of gonzo, from what we've seen ...' Kim slayed me, before we said our goodbyes on the platform.

Back to the other side. Back to Aneesha Medha at the Lakeside World Masters, Indian super fan number one who I said I'd catch up with later and here I am, sat in the time-warp Continental Hotel, which is part of the Lakeside Complex, a red-brick building that looks like an oversized Barratt semi.

Having spent a fair bit of time there, India may carry the image of a mind-fuck of a country (in all senses) at the best of times, but in actuality, it's a rather serene place if you get past the constant hassle you get off every one at every moment, and the thought of darts making a cameo appearance in this land just doesn't really make any sense. Cricket, okay, but why darts? And where would people play it?

'We don't have darts in the pubs in India. I have a set up at home and in my workplace, so whenever I get the time I throw some darts,' Aneesha tells me as we grab a table in the Continental Bar. 'And for the experience of playing I've found this website called the webcam darts association, where you can play people from all over the world,' she told me with much Indian zest.

'Isn't darts a colonial hang-over? A game of your former oppressors?' I ask somewhat glibly.

'The English have really left behind quite a lot in Kolkata,' she tells me. 'But darts only really began in India in 2002, when there were the first national championships. I started playing in 2004 and from then until now I've seen a lot of darts players coming up. It's still at a very early stage here, but we have the Darts Premier League of India that started in May last year.'

The Darts Premier League – India's first franchise-based darts tournament to be held in Kolkata – is an annual nine-team championship based around celebrity and made possible by some blatant brand sponsorship. Each darts team has a famous Tollywood star attached as an ambassador. (Tollywood is the Telugu/West Bengal cinema industry based in Hyderabad in the Indian states of Telangana and Andhra Pradesh.) The teams, and their stars, of 2016 were: Shining Stars (Rituparna Sengupta), Aauris Strikers (Tanushree Chakraborty), Apollo Arrows (Ananya Chatterjee), Tungsten Creed (Arunima Ghosh), Sharp Shooters (Gargi Roychowdhury), Warriors (Ushasie Chakraborty), Eklavya (Rachel White), Arrow Heads (Sampurna Lahiri) and Magma Yoddha (Sohini Sarkar), and each team has a brand that is never far behind it. They're not mucking around with any grassroots slow-grow-to-see-how-it-goes type of BDO business plan. No, it's straight into the mainstream and I immediately like the ambition of it, and even more the fact that each team has a compulsory five men and three women players. That's what I call progress.

'There was an auction of the local players and money was involved – and once money was in the mix a lot of people became interested in the game.'

'So they auctioned off the best players?' I quiz.

'Essentially.'

'And how does it get out there?'

'Star TV and Doordarshan.' Which is the equivalent of Sky and the BBC, which just goes to show they are taking this business seriously.

'Who is your darting hero?' I have to ask.

'I love watching Deta Hedman – she is the reason I'm playing darts.'

I spend some time wandering around the Lakeside Complex and can't help comparing my evening with what I imagine would go down in the Calcutta Gymkhana Tennis Club – one of the venues for the Darts Premier League, a place that leaves no doubt as to how anything colonial is still revered, and almost part of the class system in Kolkata today. From what Aneesha had recounted I know it has a spanking new dartboard and some very serious players, who would all beat me without breaking a sweat, even in my imaginary travels.

'There used to be this craze for imported breakfast cereal,' Aneesha told me before our interview drew to a close. 'You would hear people talking loudly about the most juvenile, sugar-saturated British and American brands.'

'Lucky charms?' I ventured.

'Ja. And Captain Crunch.' Which when said in a thick/posh/British/Indian accent sounds like the best brand in the world. 'So when you think about all this darting interest, it seems, well, it seems perfectly natural.'

She added, 'Most of the time, Indians like to lead the world, but sometimes we are so obsessed with what is happening, or what we believe to be happening – over here – that we become slaves to the next trendy-bendy idea, ja?'

'So darts blowing up in England sends a ripple of interest out there and somebody thinks it's a bandwagon to jump on.'

'Ja, and there is a quick lakh of bucks to be made.' (A lakh is a term for 100,000.)

ALICE IN CHAINS

'Tattoo, gold chain, overly big shirt.'

Alice defines your average darts player

A few days later, thankfully, everything calms down for a while, and you find me sat in the bedroom of Alice, in a village near Henley, in the Royal County of Berkshire – Moneyville, in other words. On the wall opposite her bed there is a huge LCD screen tuned to Sky Sports. The darts is on. Alice is a fresh and healthy eighteen-year-old personal trainer and definitely not your average darts fan, but then again I've been told many times on this journey that there is no such thing as an average darts fan and it's about time I started listening. Alice is the future of darts.

There is a pub down the road from the fitness centre where she works and if her sessions are cancelled – which they often are as her main clientele are the rich, bored housewives of Henley – she wanders down with her colleagues to throw some darts. On top of this, her best friend religiously goes to the World's, and last year Alice wanted to know what the fuss was about and started watching darts on her big flat screen when she was lolling about at home. 'I knew it was all about getting drunk and not actually seeing the darts – but after ten minutes or so I was really into it and watched it every night from that moment on.'

If you can sell the idea of darts to someone like Alice, then you can sell it to anyone. The $64million question is how she, a personal trainer, gets past the truly abysmal health profile of most of the players.

'I think it's what darts is. They started playing by going to the pub every night, drinking and playing darts. I think that's where they got the image from. People don't look at darts and say, "That's a good sport; I'm going to train for that!" They go to the pub at eighteen, play darts and get drunk. Then comes the stuff like all the tattoos and all the gold necklaces …'

Alice has a darts routine. She tunes in when it starts and keeps one semi-interested eye on the walk-ons and interviews and everything at the beginning. 'I'll be on my phone and stuff but when they start throwing the darts I properly watch it.' She finds the after-game interviews reasonably interesting but she just wants to watch them play darts. 'Like get into it.' Which means a lot in this day and age.

And when it comes to event branding, the crazy thing is that Alice doesn't even notice the sponsors, because – thanks to the design or the category or semiotics – they just don't register on the brain of an eighteen-year-old girl from southern England. It's a demographical hole. 'But I feel like I'm the odd one out as everyone else is going to be betting on the darts.'

Before she had a first-hand view of the sport, Alice thought it was just for fat old men to watch when they were hiding from their wives in the pub, drinking and the like, but 'as soon as I started watching it, I loved it ...'

Sadly, Alice's female peers don't share her enthusiasm, as on the night of the 2017 semi-final she was invited to go and hang at a friend's house. 'I was like – the darts is on, I can't come, and they were like – why are you watching the darts over coming to us? I was like – it's the darts final I'm not missing it, but I'll come if you let me watch it at your house, and they were like – that isn't happening, and I was like – I'm not coming then, I'll see you tomorrow. They just don't get it.'

I – like – love that eighteen-year-old suburban vernacular, and the Nando's culture it was born out of as that's the future of darts.

DARTING JESUS

'Every year we get people dressed as Superman, Spiderman, Thunderbirds and nuns coming to the World Championship, and the punters in fancy dress add to the fantastic atmosphere of the occasion. I see no reason why we should not let a bloke who looks like Jesus enjoy the spectacle – as long as he observes the rules like everybody else. If Clark Kent, Peter Parker, Virgil Tracy or Mother Teresa misbehaved, they would be thrown out, and the same applies to 'Jesus'.

Phil 'The Power' Taylor

This chapter wouldn't be complete without mentioning Nathan Grindal. Who? You probably won't know who he is – unless I say 'Darting Jesus'.

A few years ago Nathan went to the darts and got the fans so worked up – as everyone thought he looked like Jesus and began to chant his biblical name – that he got asked to leave or calm down or both. He promised to behave and not ham it up, but then couldn't help himself. It began to put the players off, which is a little hard to believe as the darts is hardly a quiet place, but that's what they said and he was warned again and given another chance.

What happened? He walks in to the 2013 Cash Converters Players Championship at the Minehead Butlin's and gives it the whole Jesus thing – arms spread, palms upturned, the beard, the halo, the works. The place went nuts and rightly or wrongly Nathan 'Jesus' Grindal got chucked out on his ass by the security.

'Two big beef-head security guards dragged me into an office and told me they wouldn't let me watch the darts. I felt quite intimidated. The head of security told me they would not be letting me into the tournament as they didn't want a repeat of last year. It's not my fault that I look like Jesus,' Nathan told the *Daily Mirror* afterwards.

I spent a couple of minutes tracking him down on the internet and then found him alive and well and spreading his gospel via Facebook and Twitter, although he didn't respond to me on either. It took a while to get through with a bombardment of messages, and posts on his timeline, as Nathan seemed a bit reluctant to talk about what happened. But then I sent him a final, grown-up, message giving him the official right to reply as I have got the PDC version of events, and then we began a drawn-out conversation via Facebook chat, which ended up with Nathan asking me how much money I would pay him for the interview, which hardly motivated me.

I offered to take him out for a night of food and drink – which he wasn't interested in, but then I reckon offering a meal to a man who can feed the 5,000 does seem a little miserly … He ended up asking for £500 and when I said I would run it past my editor, he pointed out that was £500 per hour. Whatever way you look at it, Jesus or not, he was taking the piss. I pointed out to Nathan that he was acting like Jesus on the payroll (an obscure Balearic beats reference), to which he responded that his name was Nathan Grindal (which I already knew from adding him on Facebook). So perhaps he had had a humour by-pass before he left his antipodean homeland.

When I spoke to Magic Dave from the PDC about Darting Jesus he made a face. 'We gave him another chance, and let him back in, on his word that he would behave and not do the whole 'Jesus thing'. First thing he does when he gets in was the whole 'Jesus thing' and the crowd go wild then – after he gets thrown out – and sells his story to a news agency …'

Which for me is the lowest of the low. And this is where we shall leave Jesus behind. At least he made a few quid.

The security at the darts have their work cut out. Because of the booze and the testosterone and the general excitement, and barbarity of the event, things do tend to get out of hand. It's inevitable when the business model is based on booze and blokes and more booze. And when I say out of hand, I mean rowdy as fuck. These bouncers don't muck around – fast forwards to the guy (who turned out to be an internet prankster) running onto the stage at the 2017 World's and grabbing the trophy. I followed the security as they dragged him outside and he was crying in pain when they had him in a choke hold. 'You're killing me,' he screamed.

'It's unfortunate that things like that happen because he's never going to watch a live darts game in his life again …' said Michael van Gerwen. 'He said to me, "Just take the trophy now cos you're gonna win it anyway", and it was very kind of him but it broke my concentration. Not only mine but Gary stopped playing very well, you have to make sure you keep performing from that moment. You've got it in football you get it in darts when people try to be funny but …'

Interlude #5 – A darts lesson with Devon in Somerset

> *'The Press Office will be located in the Crazy Horse Room, based near one of the entrances to the Skyline Pavilion. Press can collect their press pass from the PDC ticket collection desk in the Crazy Horse foyer – doors open one hour before each session begins.'*
>
> From the PDC press pack

I drive to what seems like the end of the world – which Minehead Butlin's is when compared to my usual Soho haunts – and when I wander around the place I realise that I couldn't actually be any further from my usual points of cultural references either. The 2016 Cash Converters Players Championship at Butlin's is awash in a sea of cheap booze – four huge tanks of beer are stacked high like giant Lego blocks by the entrance, flanked on either side by fast food outlets – burgers to the left and pizza to the right – and it's as I wander into the main darts arena I'm finally struck by the power of the darts. There are five thousand revellers chugging back two-pint glasses of bright yellow lager and chanting and singing and dancing and praying at the altar of arrows. The booze is kept flowing by young girls in tiny pink vests, who are known as 'Bar Angels' (the vest has that printed across the bust and '4 pints for £16 on the back'), running about frantically. I pass a guy sat right at the front on a red mobility scooter with a traffic cone on his head, a burger in one hand and a bucket of lager in the other … Darts is certainly inclusive. The nubile Bar Angels cannot bounce the drinks out quick enough, and so there is a constant trail of pink tracking back and forth from the bar – every surface of which is rammed with four-pint jugs that can't be filled quick enough – and the punters in the arena are howling for more.

Later I overhear that the Saturday-night bar will take in excess of £100K.

An obese twenty-something guy waddles past rocking an 'I beat anorexia' T-shirt and eating a pizza out of the box. Two of the Beatles – Sgt Pepper era – run past as if they are on a timer, and I instinctively follow them … to the bookies where they hastily slap down bets.

'Who you betting on?' I ask, but get totally blanked as apparently if you talk about the bet it somehow queers your luck. I watch Ringo and John run back to their seats with a flea in my ear. For some reason I begin to think about pizza. And beer.

Whilst surveying the landscape I realise that the world I have come from is so obsessed with the progress of one's career, and that the people enjoying themselves in the Butlin's Minehead may be a dying breed – salt of the earth. At least they know what they want, what they are after, and how to get it. For this long weekend they can forget the night shift, the gas bill, the need for a new carburettor or whatever, and chug and sing and dance and – perhaps most importantly – snatch a moment of glory in TV land, which they will be recording at home just in case they indeed reach Nirvana and need to share that glorious moment as a snapshot from the box through their social media stream.

I flounder around for a while taking in the madness, before Magic Dave, the PDC media manager, appears and takes pity on me. 'You want a tour?' he asks.

Magic Dave's tour has a calming influence and instantly stops me from wanting to invest in and ingest a series of four-pint jugs. The main area of the Butlin's big top has been specially converted into a darts arena with jumbotron screens hanging down, the usual long tables in the middle, and some stadium-style seating around three sides to get an extra 1,000 or so bums on seats. All built around a massive stage, next to which is a walk-on ramp for the players to parade along with the walk-on girls. All this is going out live on ITV4 or some such freeview digital cul-de-sac.

Dave takes me to the second stage, which is outside the main zone in the 'Reds' club. It's a lot darker and instantly takes me back to the olden days of the Circus Tavern, before Barry got involved.

'It's more of a club atmosphere in here,' Dave tells me.

'And you can almost touch the players!' I offer.

'Exactly, but don't tell them that!' We wander around and as I try to enter the main arena the automatic doors refuse to open and I plough head-first into the security glass. 'We had to turn them off as they were interfering with the darts!' Dave tells me.

'Fuck off!' I think he's winding me up.

'Straight up. The automatic doors were creating a magnetic interference with the darts when they opened and shut.'

'I can feel an interference with the force ...' I quote Darth Vader, rubbing my head. Dave obviously isn't a Star Wars buff and suddenly he has to get back to his work.

As we walk back to the media room, I ask Dave about my access to van Gerwen and discover that the world's number one doesn't want to talk to me or go on the record – apparently back in Holland there have been a couple of books about him written from such interviews.

It's as I sit back in the Crazy Horse lounge, eating a pizza (deep-pan pepperoni) that I spot a woman holding up a sign on the ITV4 live feed that states 'I'm not drinking today' in one hand and a pint in the other. Then the crowd sings that ever-present anthem again and I turn to the media person next to me and ask him what the song is.

'"Chelsea Dagger" by The Fratellis,' he erroneously tells me.

'Is it licensed?' I ask but no one knows. I think I will have to track the band down to discover if they know they are so popular round these parts.

One thing that's struck me is that these darts hacks think I'm a weirdo. I can tell. Just as it's about to get really awkward, Devon Petersen walks into the place to get his wristband and I jump up and literally run over to introduce myself. We've been having a two-month-long Twitter exchange, but today's the day we meet in the flesh. We wander out into the cold wet drizzly afternoon and as soon as we get near the main entrance, Devon is pretty much besieged by selfie requests, which have replaced the old-school autograph.

Back in the Reds club stage Devon and I watch Joe Cullen thrash John-Boy Robie (not his real name but I liked the hickiness of it) 6–0 and then we wander back to their chalet, which is like a teenager's student room but with a dartboard by the window and cans of Kopparberg spilling out of its case. Homely.

'You need a glass?' Devon offers and it's at this point I realise I'm carrying a four-pint jug of lager, which we begin to drink from, whilst catching up about all things South African. What I have to explain here is that both Devon and I consider South Africa home. We avidly chat about Mitchells Plain, Gatsbys, biltong, N1 City and other assorted South Africanisms. Joe the Conqueror comes in and makes a pan of instant spicy rice/shit pasta from a packet and flops next to me on the Butlin's sofa (designed to be so uncomfortable that it makes you get up off your arse and get back into one of the many pubs and bars and drop some hard-earnt cash) and eats it straight out of the pan, which is always an endearing sight. It's almost a teenage ritual and a show of supreme confidence, which Joe needs on his sky-bound trajectory. Plus he's in a good mood after his whitewash. I like him immediately.

Then, with a Nescafe sachet for an oche, Devon and I play some solid darts.

'You've got a nice throw,' Devon informs me, which is the first ever professional compliment about my game. He then wants to know what darts I use as we both have the South African flag as flights.

'*Cheap ones!*' *is the answer. He examines them and nods to say 'they will do fine for you' and we play on. This is my first ever game with a professional, and he's such a decent fella that I feel myself playing better because I'm in a perfect darts mindset with a legend in the making, but I still have to ask:*

'*I really need some help with my darts!*'

'*I can see that!*'

And the following six minutes is a master class in darts devastation. By the time I've got my score down to around the 400 mark, Devon is checking out on a double something. I'm not joking, and I can feel that this is the start of a pattern. In a darts sense I feel almost naked and at the same time so annoyed that my darts are not going where I want them. I hit a 20 and Devon kindly applauds.

'*You just need to keep practising. Like really hard.*'

'*Any other tips?*'

'*I'm not sure what else I can suggest. How long do we have?*'

And it's then I realise that one part of this darting mission is going to be harder than the rest of it. I pack my darts up and get ready to make the long schlep back to London, if only I could remember where I'd parked the car.

CHAPTER SIX

THE WOMEN

'I can hold my own against any good player and to actually beat the male professionals was wonderful, just wonderful. I love to beat any man.'

Maureen Flowers, number-one female darts player
of the 1970s and '80s, and ex-wife to Eric Bristow

After spending a fair bit of time in and around the BDO, the most interesting side of it, when examined through my wonky gonzo lens, was most definitely the women. The youth system seemed as chaotic as the day-to-day BDO, where the men's seemed plain irrelevant, especially compared to the skill and level of competition in the PDC. The fact that most of the up-and-coming PDC youth players could probably win any of the major BDO tournaments said it all. I would obviously like to put that to the test and I know Barry would be up for lending me a player or two, but I'm still waiting to hear back from Sue Williams at the BDO about a number of things.

I had a hard time getting my head around why anyone cared about second-division players, so I was drawn to the women right from the start. Okay, so in the PDC the women's role is exclusively played out on screen by Daniella and Charlotte – the walk-on girls – or Laura Woods as an interviewer for Sky Sports, and apart from the nice lady who made me a cup of tea when I got to the PDC HQ, it was totally a blokey geezer-freezer affair.

The real diehard fans that I met, at the BDO and the PDC, were all women. On both sides of the game, the men were more interested in the peripheral aspects of the game and didn't actually give that much of a toss about the actual sport. They were there for the other reason. The stag-do without the wedding. The crack without the pipe. No one I spoke to seemed that bothered about individual players, and this was compounded when I was watching the Women's World Championship finals and noticed that Martin Adams was paying more attention to his phone than the game in hand. Which might seem like I'm just building them up to knock them down, but I was there watching and that was what happened.

The more time I spent in the Lakeside players' bar (which handily doubled as the practice area) the more I realised that the most interesting and progressive side to all of this is the women's game. Who, I may add, play for a tenth of the prize money as the BDO men and a thousandth of the PDC men. They're just as good at darts and they play a totally different game, which seems to rely a lot more on exploiting your opponent's mistakes than focusing on your own successes. I stood right in front of the Lakeside stage and watched Lisa Ashton win the World Championship and she did this because she constantly hit her target and whenever her opponent made a mistake Lisa punished her for it.

'Come on, Mum!' Danielle Ashton shouted at every opportunity, some of my favourite moments during my entire adventure. It represented family, support, loyalty, the tight-knit community of the BDO – compared to the cold cash machine of the PDC. I could stand there and actually watch Lisa's darts hit the board and hear her curse when they failed to go where she wanted them to go. Or hear her gee herself up when they hit their target.

'There is a real family community in the BDO, and you can take your family and feel comfortable. I wouldn't feel secure taking Danielle to the PDC or owt,' Lisa told me afterwards in the bar as she celebrated with her friends and family. Her voice was going, but she managed to talk to me for a moment longer. I asked her about the battle of the sexes. 'The standard we're playing at the moment is better than the men. The women's standard is going higher and higher and we're playing better than the men, and there is no one I dread to play because everyone is beatable.'

I hope to bust the myth that women can't play in the PDC. The very first woman who actually played in the PDC 2000 Skol World Championship was a lady called Gayle King from Canada. She won the first set against Graham Stoddart, and I bet he shat himself.

'I have to say the highlight of my career was stepping onto the stage at the Circus Tavern and participating in that history-making event,' said Gayle during a news report from the time. 'It had always been a dream of mine to play an event such as that and at that moment my dream came true. I will always treasure that.'

The question that is plaguing me is: how come all the top PDC players are men and none are women?

Women have been playing darts since the game began, but only 'officially' since 1958 when the National Darts Association of Great Britain introduced the first Women's Pairs Competition (won by Joan Adams and Rose Branham), and it wasn't until a few years later in 1967 that the Women's Individual Championship was established and the title claimed by the splendidly named Marjorie Drabble. I'm not sure why, but women's darts has never been taken seriously by the sponsors, which means it will never be pushed as hard into the mainstream of TV land without the commercial justification. This is all complete bollocks as I've spent a lot of time mooching around the oche with the finest women's players in the world and they are just as good as any man. Okay, so the top PDC players are in a different league and they are all men (for now) but that isn't the norm.

With the formation of the BDO in 1973 came the first proper recognition of women's darts, presenting both sexes to the world on an (almost) even footing, and the BDO's structure for county darts has always included women from the get-go. Olly Croft may have behaved like a bit of a dictator but at least he included the women of the darting world in his empire. The prize money for women at the 2017 BDO World Championship was still pretty pathetic at £12,000 when compared to the men's £100,000.

TRINA'S STORY

'Trina craved the pure glory and the self-fulfilment that becoming a champion darter would bring. This attitude is admirable; in my experience the male greats, from Alan Evans down to Phil Taylor, were always carefully watching the cash flow as well as the gong collection. They were as proud as anyone in their achievements, but were helped as television and sponsorship cash came flowing in to bulk up the rewards of the early exhibition circuit and money races. The furnace of ladies' darts is not hot enough to provide great entertainment. Now if there were 23 more Trinas on the go ...'

Sid Waddell

Cheddar Gorge was flooded when I got there way too early and so I wandered up the hill from the Riverside Inn. Due to the rain from Storm Angus that has been battering the country, the river the inn sat beside looked like it was about to burst its banks and the tourist attractions and trinket shops were all closed due to flooding, but I didn't know this until I schlepped up the top of the hill to kill half an hour and freeze my ass off, feet soaking wet thanks to my totally unsuitable footwear. When I squelched up there I could see a huddle of National Trust OAP workers sweeping and shovelling the wet gravelly debris in their yellow, pink and green neon hi-vis vests with the little acorn logo on, like a gang of elderly delinquents putting in their hours for community service. It's only as I walked back down towards the inn that I started worrying about the abundance of fast-flowing water – hoping that it stayed back and I didn't get stuck there as my car was parked at the bottom of the gorge. It was a strange sensation to be in close proximity to such a force, both the cloudy rushing high-powered river and the world's greatest female darts player, who was waiting for me in the saloon bar of the inn, where 'I'll Find My Way Home' by Jon & Vangelis was playing when I walked in.

'It's not a real memory for me, but I apparently threw my first dart, aged two, stood on a barstool in my mum and dad's pub – but obviously I can't remember that,' Trina Gulliver remembered after we sat down in a corner of the inn with a steaming pot of tea. Trina was drinking Guinness and black, the pub in her reminiscing was the Bowling Green pub in Southam, Warwickshire, located in the middle of the high street of the small Midlands village, which her parents used to run. Almost picturesque in a tea-and-scones kind of way, but still a little adrift in the suburban wilderness of the Midlands, and the place where Trina spent her first four years and began her darting journey, earlier than most, and ended up as the most successful female player ever, winning the BDO World Championship ten times.

You can almost hear the arrows flying through the air towards the faded and punctuated board, and imagine a young Trina wandering around her parents' pub and interacting with the punters in a way that only a small cute child in a boozer can get away with. This was the genesis of her darting journey, those smells and noises and interactions and landscape that can only be described as British and can be only found in a pub.

'I'm the youngest of five so my first real memory is being at home with a dartboard, as we all played darts at some point in time at some sort of level. And Mum and Dad being in the pub trade there was this natural progression.'

Then her parents got divorced, and Trina stopped playing darts. It was almost like there was an unconscious connection between the darts and the pub, and the pub and her parents, and after this massive upheaval, something had to give, and that could be why she stopped playing darts and allowed woodwork and joinery to take over. For the next decade, when Trina wasn't at school or playing with her friends, she was always sawing, hammering, joining pieces of wood of various sizes and this concentrated effort must have improved her hand-to-eye coordination (Phil Taylor made toilet chain handles, John Lowe was also a carpenter), because when she picked up a dart again some years later she was completely unstoppable.

'At about fourteen I would go and sit in the corner of the Bowling Green pub with my lemonade and watch my sisters play for the youth team. Afterwards I would start practising and someone from the team would give me a game, and that's when I began to get properly into it.'

It's now that I begin to wonder – out loud – about what makes darts so special?

'I think ultimately it's because it's a social thing that you do in a pub – you meet people, play, have a drink … It can quickly become a bug …' Trina offered.

'But can anyone play?' I asked, ever hopeful.

'You need a bit of a natural talent for it, and the rest comes with dedication and practice and commitment. A lot of it is down to mental attitude, as with any sport, but there is a lot more in darts than people realise. You don't just have to throw a dart. You need your calculation – obviously – which to be fair sometimes I struggle with, but it's a lot about the mental attitude and concentration levels, and that's something you can't teach. It has to come naturally.'

Talk turns to the difference between the PDC and the BDO – a subject never far away in the world of darts.

'The PDC is far rowdier than the BDO. The BDO is still noisy but it's how you get your focus and nerves to work for you and not against you. You have to get in that zone.' Often events in your personal life can affect how you play on the board, because that's when you can't focus. 'If your mind isn't completely focused then you can let stuff in –

like the washing machine is on the blink …' And it's details like this
that make the game of darts such a normal sport. An everyday sport.

Trina is a full-time darts player, but still does the occasional bit of
joinery. In the past she's worked eighteen-hour shifts as a carpenter,
and then still had to get out there and play some killer darts. 'We've
all been there; we've all done that as you don't get the rewards if you
don't put the effort in.'

Trina has been in the world of darts since she was fourteen, and this
is a deep-assed journey which really cements her place in the history of
the BDO. 'I started off in the youth system, which came under the BDO
banner, and I've got a lot of respect for Olly. I came up through the
county system. When I did the first Warwickshire Youth Open, I was
fourteen and the landlord – who had taken over from her parents – at the
Bowling Green talked me into entering and he paid for me to enter and
my dad took me to Coventry and I went and won both girls and boys.'

After that Jack Cundy – the manager of the Warwickshire youth
team – asked Trina to play for them. There was a moment when he
sat her down and told her that if she continued to play as well as she
was, that she would go on to play for England. He was spot on with his
prediction, although sadly Jack had died before he could see it happen.

'It was 1994, I remember the date as it was the same year I got
married and at that time I was just so confused.' And if there is anyone
in darts that's been confused, it's Trina.

The media have always looked down on darts because of where it
all originated from, and until the sport is totally reborn (and perhaps
that is well on the way to actually happening) it's always going to have
the smell of the pub attached to it, although things are looking brighter.
'People look back at that period when it was massive in the 1980s, and
that is how a lot of people remember it. There was a massive stigma
attached then because of the smoking and drinking onstage. And now
it's very different, it's a much cleaner image, but people don't see this.'

'But what about the kids who are now playing, who haven't come
out of the pub, who don't even drink?' I asked.

'They are still all coming out of the pub one way or another. Where do you play? Where do practise? Play super league? The pub is part of the growing tree.'

So the journey is thus: local pub, local league. Then super league. Then maybe if you have the skills to pay the bills you can play for England or Scotland or Wales or Northern/Ireland. Up until recently all the PDC players have pretty much graduated from the pub.

'People will always look at how much players like van Gerwen earn and want some of that . . .' I offered.

'Yeah. Where d'you think he came from?' Trina asked.

'The BDO!' I said, working it all out on my own. 'But how far has the game taken you?' I divert the conversation somewhat.

'When I started it was initially only the UK as that was all I could afford. I didn't have the sponsors – I entered the open tournaments, but up to today I've been fortunate to travel all over the world. To be honest, you never get to see anywhere you go as it's airport, venue, win or lose, back to the hotel and before you know it you're on the plane back home.'

Trina's first foreign trip was the Swiss Open and she took her mum who had just lost her husband. Trina got into the semis in the singles, but she also tried her hand in the pairs with a Danish player called Gerda Stoddard and they won it! But despite the win, Trina still returned from Basel out of pocket as the prize money didn't even cover her expenses. She knew that if she was to really get somewhere, she had to get out there both nationally and internationally and this was going to cost.

'I've been to Australia and Vegas a few times. Malaysia, Singapore, but mainly Europe. The Desert Classic is out in Vegas run by the PDC. It's a different world, and Vegas was one of the rare places where you do get some time off. I flew over the Grand Canyon in a helicopter and threw up everywhere in the back. I left a little bit of myself in the Grand Canyon.'

Now, I'm a queer fellow and the world of darts is still a strange manly world, not really known for its openness and inclusivity, and

I can't help thinking back to the comment made (okay, so it was said as a joke with absolutely no malice whatsoever) by Michael van Gerwen in the Wolverhampton press office, when he told the fresh-faced PDC camera boy that he was looking very gay. And if this is someone being funny then my mind boggles when I think about the realities of actually being gay in the world of darts – both PDC and BDO – and how not only the fans but the sponsors (mostly gambling and other low-end services) pump some serious cash into the sport. How would the *Sun* or Cash Converters relate to a player who isn't heterosexual?

It doesn't stop there. The week after I interviewed Trina, Eric Bristow managed to push darts back onto the front page, but for all the wrong reasons. It was widely reported in the press that Eric had made a series of comments via his Twitter account suggesting that the latest football sex abuse victims were not 'proper men', bizarrely and erroneously referring to a paedophile as a 'poof'.

From @ericbristow MBE Twitter feed:

Might be a looney but if some football coach was touching me when I was a kid as i got older i would have went back and sorted that poof out.

Darts players tough guys footballers wimps.

Bet the rugby boys are ok ha ha

U got to sought him out out when u get older or don't look in the mirror glad i am a dart player proper men'

Eric was subsequently fired from his Sky TV commentator role, and I instantly made up my mind not to interview him for this book; I had to fight my instinct to go back and erase all traces of him in some kind of Stalinist fashion. Following his outburst, Bristow then appeared on Good Morning Britain and following a combative exchange with Piers Morgan, admitted it was 'a miswording' and apologised for calling these victims wimps. Whether this apology is accepted is not my concern; suffice to say he still seems to get regular exhibition bookings.

There was a moment back in time when Trina sat down and convinced herself she was on the wrong path. That she was living a lie. 'Do you know what, I was with my husband for eighteen years, and then it just went to the wall – nothing to do with him, totally my fault – because of my feelings, which totally blew me out of the water,' Trina recalled. 'I couldn't help thinking, What are you doing? Why are you feeling okay about all of these feelings when it's clearly not right, if you see what I mean? But I just couldn't help them and admitting that to myself, that I was actually gay, was a major, major, turn in my life …'

Once Trina had come to terms with who she was, then the fear of telling everyone else – her friends, her family, her sponsors – took over, as all she would have been thinking was: Oh my God, this could completely change my life in every sense and every direction. My career, friends and family: everything. 'It was massive, massive pressure and I had the balls to do it all in the end. But it was so hard.'

At moments like that, when you are in the unfathomable depths of confusion, at those times you are just scared of losing everything and everyone around you. When you are right in there you never really know how people are going to react. You know deep down that if they are not happy with what you are telling them then they are not a true friend. You are scared of losing everything because of how you are. Because you're gay.

Trina was in Holland hanging out with one of her best mates, Andy Fordham aka the Viking – who at one point would drink a full case of Holsten Pils before throwing a dart. ('I'm not proud of it but I was good at drinking … People don't believe it, but when I won the World Championship, I don't remember leaving the hotel, I don't remember getting to the venue, going on stage, nothing. I don't remember getting the trophy.') A lot of people on the circuit must have had their gaydars working – as Andy turned to Trina and said, 'When are you going to tell your mum?'

'I was like *what?*'

'You've gotta tell her you're gay before she hears it from anybody else. Because everybody knows!'

Trina is the greatest female darts player and now happily married to Sue, who I've had the honour of having a drink with in the Lakeside players' bar. Considering how straight and white and backward looking the BDO appears to be, I have to take my hat off to its openness and inclusivity towards anyone who isn't heterosexual. It's easy to shoot it down (the internet is a good place for people to troll stuff they don't like, just take a look at the BDO's Facebook page) for being backward and run like a local scout group, but it's hard, near on impossible, to create an all-inclusive atmosphere where everyone is welcome. The BDO has that in buckets and that is what gives it a fair few points over the PDC. I know it's supposedly not a competition, but we all know it is. Remember Barry's classic quote a while back:

'Now I'm going to fuck you …'

BACK-A-YARD

'I thought you were going to be a tall black guy …'

Deta's words when we finally meet

When I open my eyes I find I'm in a Caribbean paradise. No, not an all-in resort where you can simply raise a little flag and the local dreadlock brings you a drink (domestic spirits and local beer only), but a rural community high up in the village of Castleton, in the parish of St Mary. Chooks and goats and wild dogs roam about, pecking and clucking and growling at each other. Plumes of grey smoke waft in and out of the colonial stoops as the day progresses and the heat rises and the back kitchen fires burn low and slow.

'You had an underground hole in the dirt that was basically an oven with a big stone and coals. It would take hours to cook anything …'

The hours marked out by the almost endless list of chores that everyone had to fulfil. And into this scene wandered a little girl. She was allowed to play in the front of the house – the kind of dwelling that had a hole dug in the shade of the back yard with a big chunk of ice wrapped in a cloth that served as a fridge and a cooler, and a hole in a lean-to on the back of the house to cook in. She remembers the brightness and the canopies of the trees and the fact that she had to work the land like the rest of her family.

'My life in Jamaica: you had to work, you had your chores that you had to do every day before you go to school, which was only four days a week. Friday we had to go to the farm and harvest what was ready, so my aunt could go to the market Friday evening and try to sell everything she's got and buy things like sugar and salt fish that would last all week. We lived off the land basically.'

Deta was born in Jamaica, in the town of Harbour View, which sits in the parish of St Thomas, and moved with her family to a small village in Essex at the age of fourteen.

'Oh God, when I arrived it was the thirty-first of January and it was so cold I nearly died. Oh my God. But it was exciting because it was a new world, y'know ...'

I was sat backstage of the Lakeside Country Club catching up with Deta Hedman. Well, I was having a drink and she was throwing arrows, warming up for her next match, but even so it was a relaxed moment as she kindly wound the reels of her history back in time for me. Deta is currently the world number 2 women's player in the BDO league, and I wasn't going to ask her to play me; giving me a severe thrashing is not going to improve her game. Plus this area is for players only and even though I had my darts on me I knew they wouldn't be doing any flying. Like Trina, Deta supped a pint of Guinness and black (the drink of choice for the women players) and threw with the precise fierceness of a champion player – in the Fred Trueman sense of the word. Reet champion.

After a while she had her arm in and we wandered out into the main room. Although she is such a recognisable player (there is only one

MAIN MEALS

STEAK & ALE PIE	£9.50
JUMBO COD	£9.00
CURRY OF THE DAY	£8.00
VEGETARIAN OPTIONS	£7.50
ALL THE ABOVE SERVED WITH FRIES OR RICE OR SALAD	
SAUSAGE & CHIPS	£7.50
BURGER & CHIPS	£8.00

HALF CHICKEN	£7.50
BOX OF FRIES	£4.00

12 PORTION PIZZA ____ £16.00 (FRIES EXTRA)

SNACKS

BURGER IN BUN	£5.50
HOT DOG ROLL	£5.00
BOX OF CHIPS	£4.00
CHEESY CHIPS	£5.00
JACKET POTATO (FILLED)	£6.50
SAVOURY PASTRY	£4.00

ALL SWEETS ____ £4

CASH ONLY

Top: The BDO crew: Olly Croft with Barbara Leitch, wife of Bob Potter, and Andy Fordham in 2004.

Left: The Lakeside menu – something for everyone.

Bottom right: 'True connoisseurs of darts' enjoying the BDO World Championships in 2015.

Top left: Barry Hearn in 1992, around the time the PDC was established.

Top right: Your esteemed auth with a very accommodating Barry Hearn in 2016.

Middle: A lively bunch applau Jelle Klaasen's arrival at the PD World Championships in 2015

Bottom: Jocky Wilson on his way to the semi-finals of the World Championships in 1984

Top: Grown adults dressed as crayons.

Middle: "Make darts great again" Trump is in town and amongst the punters at Ally Pally.

Bottom: Eric Bristow apologises on Good Morning Britain for sharing his views regarding paedophilia on twitter.

Top: Phil 'The Power' Taylor wins the 1995 PDC World Championship and a cheque for £12,000.

Middle: Martin 'Wolfie' Adams and Trina Gulliver celebrate their BDO wins in 2011.

Bottom: Nathan Grindal: the Jesus of darts.

Top: South African Devon Petersen in the 2017 PDC World Championship.

Middle: 'The Dark Destroyer' Deta Hedman, representing England, sporting the colours of Jamaica.

Bottom: Corey Cadby of Australia made his PDC World Championship debut in 2017.

Top: A young Michael van Gerwen pops up on the Wall of Fame in the Lakeside players' bar.

Bottom: Slowly the mainstream brands are beginning to see the potential of darts. Not bad shell suit tops, to be fair.

Top: From Portakabin to Ally Pally stage: Daniella Allfree prepares to walk-on the next wannabe World Champion.

Bottom: The Circus Tavern: glitz and glamour off the A13.

As close as the author – under the guise of Captain Haddock –
will ever get to the world stage.

other black player – Olive Byamukama from Scotland via Uganda), she seemed to walk about without too much hassle.

'What do you remember about coming to England back in the day?' I asked.

'I was fourteen and excited like a kid in the candy shop. Everything was new and each day was about what I would discover next!'

'That must have been crazy?'

'Back in Jamaica everyone just had black hair, and so I caught myself staring at all the different colours and kinds of hair – people were like "what are you looking at?" and I was like "I've never seen somebody who looked like you before!"' Deta reminisced.

'Perhaps they were thinking the same thing! You just got it in first! It must have been so fucking cold?'

'When I first saw snow I had to go out there and pick it up and rub it in my face for the first time. Back in Jamaica we used to have to buy a block of ice and put it in a hole to make it last … So snow was something else.

'I didn't really get on with my dad when I came here. I didn't know him as when he came to England I was two, so I didn't really remember what he even looked like. All I had was a picture with my mum sitting in a chair and my dad standing.'

'So it took a while to settle in?'

'Everything for me was so strange. So strange. I went to an ordinary secondary school, and although we spoke English in Jamaica it was Patois, so when I got to England it took a while for me to understand what they were actually saying. Everything was really being spoken the right way – not the way we did – but getting my head around everything …' Deta pauses at the memory of trying to fit in. 'You just go with the flow, really …'

I wondered how the clash of Jamaican culture and British pub culture has produced one of the world's greatest female darts players of all time when there are very few black darts fans, let alone players.

'Pubs aren't part of black culture. But in the olden days everybody used to go to the pub on a Sunday and play darts, dominoes, card games – all the little cheese and pickle and biscuits – that's where it came from, we all loved doing that at lunchtime. And where we lived in Essex, it was such a friendly place, it really, really was. Everybody knew everybody, so that was how we got used to the whole pub thing.'

Deta's been here for forty-three years and it was the fierce darting competition she had with her brothers that helped her shape her game.

'When I came here in 1973 my brothers were already here and they had a dartboard and that's how I got into it. After school I would go down and have a little muck-about with my brothers. I could never win a leg and I would go every day after I'd done my homework until I would win a game and it just went from there. And every little bit of spare time after I'd done my chores I'd have another go. And after I left school and got a job and on Sunday when we were doing nothing I used to go and practise with my brothers ...' Deta had to force herself to get her darting skills up to be able to progress. Her brothers showed no mercy, as you'd imagine.

'But what about being a black woman in a very white male world?' It's the question I had to ask.

'Overall it's been brilliant, I'm one of those happy-go-lucky kinds of people who doesn't take any nonsense, who likes to beat the guys on the board – they totally hate that, but heigh-ho it's what it is, for me ....' Deta took another big pause where she thought about this and then took a deep, deep breath. 'It's a challenge, to be honest. And I love challenges, and if someone says to me you can't do that ... it's like a red rag to a bull as I will keep going until I can do it. That's me. Overall it's been brilliant; well, most people have been great ... But I was in Europe once and someone said, "I didn't know they trained monkeys to throw darts." It doesn't really bother me, as such. If they were to say it in my face, then I would tackle them. I would go back in their face. I will fight my battles.'

My heart sank. This is such a tragic thing to hear.

'I wear earplugs when I play because you get knobs behind me. I can still hear them but it doesn't knock you that hard – if that makes sense.' Deta opened her darts case to show me her anti-knobhead equipment.

I am ashamed to hear stories like Deta's. We walked back into the players' bar and ordered some drinks to distract ourselves from the bitter taste of deeply ingrained casual racism. Talk turns back to gender, and how the female darts players are treated by the PDC – as the divide in the game once again reared its ugly head.

'It's slightly better now but I feel we are still treated as second-class citizens. I thought the ladies PDC World Championship was a hastily thrown-together event. The top ladies sent over some ideas that we thought would attract a class entry into the event. However, the PDC totally ignored our ideas and a lot of the girls didn't enter, as they'd adopted a wait-and-see attitude.' Deta played in the PDC side when they opened it up to women in 2010. 'I only really played as I would drive my ex, Colin Lloyd (darts player formerly ranked number one and nicknamed 'Jaws'), to the events and thought I might as well have a go. I loved it. I had some good wins – especially when I thrashed Wes Newton on his own patch. I've never been scared of playing men, why should I be?'

'In darts you are all equal!' I offered, loving the idea of a Jamaican-born female darts player slaying some arrogant English male. True revenge.

'Try telling the men that! I can remember years ago in the Harlow Open when I was about to play Kevin Painter in the semi-final, and overheard him saying to his mate John McFall that when he beat me to get in the final they would split the money. Fired me up shit loads and I not only beat Kevin in the semi-final but John in the final too ...' Bang! These are the stories that need telling through a high-definition reconstruction with a huge budget shot by Danny Boyle.

'How was it when you started playing in the PDC?' I asked.

'We weren't sure why they wanted us there.' The inclusion of female players in the PDC was short lived, and soon they dropped the idea altogether. 'I believe that if the event was repeated the turnout would be very good. The top players like myself, Tricia Wright and the other BDO ladies put themselves on the line for this event. We were well up for it, but it didn't work out as we wanted.'

'I'll be seeing Barry Hearn soon at one of his big events, I'll pass on your message,' I told her. 'He may let you women back in!'

Deta laughed, and I don't know if it's because she thought that was funny or because she felt that I'd be wasting my time. 'To be fair, there is nothing stopping a woman from joining the PDC: they can still play. It's there, but they haven't specifically put anything out there. If you are a lady you just have to take a chance with the guys as well. Whereas with the BDO you have the men and the ladies but the reward is not that great. If the money was there I would have gone full time. Dedicate my time to just playing. But unfortunately it's not. I love competing anyway and it's great to travel to different countries I've never been to, and enjoying life while I can, where it takes me or not.'

But the cold harsh reality is that Deta may be the world number 2, but she still has to win matches to pay her bills. This must be one of the downsides of the BDO – the prize money isn't enough for the women players to live off.

'I'm a semi-pro, to put a finer word on it. To me, when somebody says you're a professional, that's what you do for a living. But I'm a semi-pro, because I've always worked. Once I left school I found a bedsit. From there I just worked, paid my bills, and darts is just a hobby that I thoroughly enjoy. Whenever I get prize money, I think, Okay, that's the council tax paid.' Deta has worked at the Post Office for twenty years.

This seems a little unfair when you consider how much money the men can win in the PDC competitions. 'That's why I get so angry with the World Championship, because the men's prize money is £100,000 and the ladies' is £12,000. And it's only three years ago that it went up to £12,000. Before that it was ten, and before that it was six, and before that it was four.'

My thoughts turned and my own love of Jamaican culture began to seep into the conversation. 'You still listen to reggae and eat rice and peas?'

'Where I live in Essex there are not that many black families, and being that young my brothers used to play reggae but …' Deta trailed off thinking heavily about my question. 'I really don't know what I am now – it sounds silly but as I haven't grown up in my own culture for forty-odd years, I've lost it. I was recently talking to a lady I work with at the Post Office who's from Zimbabwe and I was saying to her that there is really nothing West Indian about me, although I was born there, but I grew up in England so I'm very much more British than I am Jamaican.'

'But you still represent your heritage?'

'I still wear the Jamaican colours on my shirts as I was born there and still hold that true, and I would never get rid of that – but overall when you speak to me I'm very much British. After forty-three years living somewhere you become that way. If I was living in London I think I would have still been very much West Indian, because everybody is still surrounded by that culture. But because where I was it was very dominantly white people it kinda rubs off on you …'

I couldn't have hoped for a better darts narrative. The story of a fourteen-year-old Jamaican teenager who came to England and became one of the superstars of the BDO, with a huge following – which will only grow now she is commentating on Channel 4 – is a great rags-to-riches storyline. And when I find out that the greatest-ever darts player has never beaten her, my fandom steps up a notch. Deta is one of the incredible people of darts.

'Men are beginning to realise that we are serious. At a recent event I beat Scottish international Ewan Hyslop and English international Scott Mitchell. Earlier this year I beat Brendan Dolan 4–1 and famously I am probably the only player in the world that has a 100 per cent winning record against Phil Taylor. I beat him in a players' championship 5–0 …' Some killer darts indeed from Deta.

Interlude #6 – Beaver Las Vegas

I had to go to Los Angeles for film business and realise that I have two reasons to make a detour on the way to Las Vegas: 1) in homage to Fear and Loathing in Las Vegas, and 2) because that is where American darts is based and Las Vegas is where the next big push through the US Masters will come from. But I thought I would fly in and drive out, which was the opposite of Hunter's original adventure.

I knew a little about the place from dearest Hunter. I packed my patterned shirt, ochre-tinted Aviators, white Converse, green cargo shorts, and a natty tweed sports jacket, and stepped out . . .

. . . I knew that it was going be one of those bastard ball-ache journeys, the ones where you are up against it from the start: flying KLM via Amsterdam and Minneapolis, in order to get to Las Vegas. A customs cop begins to fuck with me in the immigration queue on landing at Minneapolis-St Paul (a place I never knew existed and will never – if there is a god – have reason to return to). My flimsy excuse for all this travelling in the middle of some very heady darts research was to meet a producer who was interested in my documentary. The fact that I'd chosen to fly out after Trump's immigration ban with a lengthy stop-over in the 'Dam (having short arms and deep pockets, therefore buying the cheapest flight) and then take on US customs and immigration deep in Bible Belt America said it all. Ten years ago with a stop-over in Amsterdam I would have most definitely spent a hectic half-hour smoking AK47 in a secret little coffee shop I had stashed ten mins away on the metro from Schiphol airport, but these days I know better and when I hit the sacred ground of the US of A I was clean as a whistle and straight as the Pope's.

So I'm standing there minding my own, when this chubby pink man with skin like Hubba Bubba in a dark blue uniform swaggers up to me and nods hello.

'All right?' I ask, not sure if I'm getting stuck up or felt up.

'You just come in on the Amsterdam flight?' He quizzes.

'Yup. From the Yew Kay (don't confuse them by saying England). It was just a connection in Amsterdam.' I'm not going to fall for that one.

'You smoke?'

'Nope.'

'Come on,' he urges. 'Everybody likes a toke now and again.' I pretend that I've suddenly caught his drift.

'I can assure you,' I say in my best English accent, 'that I most certainly do not like a "toke".'

'But you guys all take drugs, right?'

'Absolutely not!' I lie through my teeth. 'I'm a father of two!' I add.

'So your kids take drugs!' he blurts, and this is when I know I've got him.

'My kids are seven and eleven years old,' I lie. Well, they were once. 'And I take great offence at your suggestions that my beautiful and innocent young children take drugs! I am en route to meet some of the most upstanding members of the Nevada business community in relation to a most community-minded darts project.'

The word darts confuses him. He walks off and approaches a couple of young lads who have just joined the back of the queue. What could be more innocuous than darts business?

I make the connecting flight into LAS VEGAS (cue neon!) and split a cab with some absolute nutter who tries to impress me with his tales of losing a fair bit of money, which explains why he is sharing the cab.

I try to check into the Hard Rock Hotel using the little VIP office, which is quite cool (lots of air con cranked up to max) and I'm told to sit and wait for the others to arrive. My contact is a guy called Tad Allagash (okay, so I nicked the last name from Bright Lights Big City, but the first bit is real) who is a producer who has made over 100 films, who I met *a while ago when I was last in Los Angeles. Since my last film has been picked up by a US distributor, I seem a much more desirable and bankable documentary director. Tad is a pretty slick operator who just so happens to have these really rich mates that he went to school with (or so his story goes) and who would be the ideal investors for my documentary about the guy who invented the Cigarette boat – the greatest-ever powerboat favoured by all the drug smugglers in Miami. Since these guys are such 'High Rollers' (read: big losers) the hotel is supplying a whole corridor of rooms for their use, free of charge. The VIP staff (hosts) know that the high rollers are coming but won't let me near a room until they get here, as I'm seen, quite rightly, as a jakey freeloader. I soon get bored, I leave my baggage with them and go for a walk, a pursuit almost unheard of in LV.*

You wanna do what?

What I need is an insight into this:

'The US Masters is the biggest thing ever to happen to darts in North America and you do not want to miss it. The best players in the world are on the line and the cream of North American talent will fight it out for their chance to put their name down in history by toppling the giants. With all the glitz and glamour of the Las Vegas strip and the fun and electric atmosphere of the darts, this is the absolute winning combination of a trip!' Barry Hearn, from a PDC press release.

One block from the 'glitz' and 'glamour' you find the real deal LV. White trash Motel 6 with a shitty casino tacked on; well, Sellotaped on, actually. Cheap rooms for cheap gamblers. And I mean cheap. This town doesn't even have a surface to scratch beneath, or a past they want anyone to see. Uptown is downtown. And downtown is fucked. The main area with all the action is called 'downtown', now a museum for relics of faded, decrepit glory. Now the place to be is called 'The Strip' (Las Vegas Boulevard). The North Strip was the place immortalised by HST, and his spot of choice, Circus Circus, is still standing but it feels like it's about to be torn down at any given moment (and by the time you read this it could well be dust). Las Vegas means 'The Meadows' in English and that's about right. All the people visiting are just cattle for the slaughter, grazing away at the tables and slots. Just remember: the house always wins. This never changes. So why bother? Oh yes, the coke and whores!

I walk around the block, which takes a fucking age in the heat, before taking a cab to a spot called the Little Crown and Anchor Pub, which turns out to be a faux-Tudor Portakabin to the west of the old strip, right in the middle of Chinatown. It's a bizarre relic but they have a couple of dartboards and I've had the foresight to pack my darts in my checked luggage, so everything pretty much becomes normal again. What can I say? I like my home comforts. They even know what shandy is! I play some games and find that just because I've travelled a few thousand miles west to the birthplace of gonzo journalism, I am still, dear reader, shit at darts. But it keeps me out of trouble in a town where trouble is easy to find.

I get a call from Mr Allagash saying that he hoped I had a pleasant flight and that they are now driving in from the airport. I bid goodbye to the darts and my new mates and the half-eaten plate of hot wings, and whip myself back to the chilly environs of the Hard Rock Hotel VIP office.

The meeting goes badly as everyone, apart from me, wants to get completely wasted and gamble and whore and I'm just some English bloke sat there with his darts getting in the way of all of this. Sat there, 6,000 miles away from home, I realise that the only thing I can do is make my excuses, play some darts. This cheers me up no end.

I make it out onto the strip again looking for darts, and thanks to Foursquare I find a bar called the Garage, a little way east past the university, which turns out to be a gay bar with pool, darts and shuffleboard, which is just the ticket after all the bullshit heterosexual 'partying' going on back at the Hard Cock Hotel. I lay into the shandies and get a few leisurely games of darts in with a geezerbird [okay, so I'm sure that isn't *the correct term but my mind is a little shot by now and looking at my notes I can see a receipt for $63 worth of craft beer and lemonade and my scrawl that says Toni] who is pretty tidy with the darts and would have easily beaten me in a fist fight, and in-between the lashings of thrashings I make lots of new friends, especially after they find out that I'm an English writer, writing an actual book. They don't care what it is about either, and I'm happy that darts is a unique and social way to open up any moment of lag. For a non-second I feel like I've found my place in society and then someone asks me a favour and I know it's time to leave, as the beer buzz is about to overtake everything else, and that would be a travesty. Time to head back to the Hard Rock; time to equalise and re-evaluate where I want to be; time to either crawl back with my tail between my legs or just style it the fuck out.*

I wake the next morning in a Motel 6 (you can't get any lower on the hotel food chain) feeling pretty good considering how many shandies I'd quaffed. I pack my South African darts and realise that it's time for me to pick up my rental car to drive to Los Angeles and find a cab to take me to the rental satellite on the edge of the fucking desert. After I have come round enough to work the controls, I take a swift detour to check out the Tropicana, the venue for the US Masters in July 2017, which was a cabaret-heavy venue with a catch phrase of 'Laugh. Rock. Magic. Tragic'. Okay, so I added an extra word. On my quick tour of the place I spot a poster for Andrew Dice Clay looking like he's actually getting younger. Painting in the attic, etc.

The one piece of the nut still left to crack is the American market. The PDC will not really be able to claim global domination in a commercial sense until they find a decent amount of traction in the North American market, which up until now has eluded them. This is probably down to a number of variables: one, the size of the country, two, the fact that darts is still pretty unknown in a country that defines sport solely through basketball, football, baseball and ice hockey, and, three, currently offers no real major financial rewards for its darts players to make a concerted effort and pull together. If you would ask me to name one American player I would draw a blank.

According to the American Darts Organization (that I read was deemed 'dysfunctional' by the American darts fans) the number one US player is Larry Butler who represents the Dart Organization of Northern Kentucky, but then much to my surprise I found that Tom Sawyer was alive and well and playing for the Minute Man Dart League. The number one women's player is Paula Murphy out of Florida who seems to pretty much win every event she plays.

The official line from the PDC is thus:

'The US Darts Masters will give North American players their chance to qualify to take on the likes of world number one Michael van Gerwen, reigning World Champion Gary Anderson and the legendary Phil Taylor onstage – with live TV coverage being shown worldwide!'

Which sounds great but the reality is that the usual PDC players will be playing each other, the only difference being that the matches are being held in a hotel in Las Vegas.

'However, in America itself,' said Magic Dave Allen, when I cornered him about the absence of yanks, 'Darin Young and Larry Butler are probably the two top players and they do make a living from playing darts, mainly around the US-based circuit but also by going to Asia. They would class themselves as professional, even though not on the PDC circuit.'

CHAPTER SEVEN

THE RISING STARS

'Michael is the boy that everyone wants to knock off so it's gonna be on his shoulders. Like they say is he going to reign as long as Phil Taylor? I don't think so because the state of darts now there are so many great darts players, he's gonna have one helluva battle for the next ten years to keep hold of everything. This young lad from Australia, he's actually told us to make the most of the next two years because he's coming, which I think is absolutely brilliant.'

> Gary Anderson, after losing in the 2017 World's
> final to MvG, name checking Corey Cadby

THE ROAD TO FAME

There are two ways of becoming a full-time darts player. One is to work your way up through local and county darts, as organised by the BDO, and the other is to go through Q-School – a brutal week of competitive darts with around 600 people going in and only thirty-two coming out with their PDC tour card. Glancing around the Q-School qualifiers in Wigan I see both boys and men trying their best to hit those trebles and go out on those doubles, players in tears, people throwing up with relief when they win … The reality is that their journey has just begun when they win their card: when they enter into the PDC as one of 128 players, the bottom 64 will lose money on the tour. It will cost them dearly. But Barry Hearn's dream is that if you can fight your way up to sixty-fourth place you will earn £50,000 and, looking at the numbers, he's not that far from achieving this. When you break it down it will probably cost the novice player £15–20,000 to play their first PDC tour, going all over Europe and wherever. The Nirvana is for the player to get into the top sixteen, where you can easily earn half a million or so, and it's a tough journey (hence the big rewards), and in a funny way, the sport has to be brutal. If it was easy to become a superstar, the whole sport would be undermined. And right now, at a time when van Gerwen is showing that he is almost unbeatable, it's a great example of what it takes to be up there with the darting stars, but also a good reminder that in the next decade or so there will surely be another van Gerwen.

'The game is professionalising year upon year upon year. The youth tour is getting better, the averages are showing that,' Leon Davis told me when I asked him about the development of the youth side of the PDC. 'Some of the youth tour and the challenge tour players would be winning BDO events with the averages they are getting. That will gradually move away as we get through the next generation of the people that weren't labourers or tradesmen running pubs. And they realise with the averages and scores that the likes of MvG and Gary Anderson are throwing constantly, they need to work hard and alcohol is not the vehicle for doing that.'

There has been a rise in the number of darting academies springing up across the UK, and this is linked to the exposure and viewing figures darts is attracting in the media and on screens both big and small and the rapidly growing prize money The next wave of emerging talent is often referred to as the 'Premier League Generation' as they have grown up watching darts on Sky TV week in and week out, they are by now sixteen or seventeen and coming to the end of their time in the youth leagues, such as the Junior Darts Corporation (JDC) – whose darting culture and references have been defined (and financed in part) by the full-whack glitz and glamour of the PDC Premier League, and they have their sights set on the money and the trappings that come with it.

And as these younger players work their way up the PDC rankings there will be a lot more professionalism, as they look better, don't drink, don't smoke and pump iron regularly, and that persona will help attract a better class of sponsors. Add to this the fact that the darting age demographic has shifted from twenty years ago when the average fan was in his fifties to today when they are now in their late twenties.

'You will see players looking after themselves more than they used to. It's important to be marketable and to attract sponsors, and there are a lot more managers in the game now who make sure the players are looking after themselves, and obviously they are all social media savvy,' Steve Brown, the chairman of the JDC, said when I sat down with him to suck out his knowledge of youth development for these very pages.

The JDC was initially started to get darts in kids' hands and to get them enjoying the sport, but over the years it has developed into a feeder system for the PDC, and it plays an important role in preparing the kids for success. There are many benefits gained from playing darts in your youth: arithmetic, social skills, learning to cope with the disappointment of losing and then fighting back from that. The general ups and downs in life, then, and the JDC seems to have filled that gap left wide open by the chaotic BDO.

'The BDO are very good at catering for the amateur darts player, who's got a mortgage, a decent job and enjoys a game of darts, and there is a place for it,' Steve said. 'And the PDC is there for the guys who want to jack their day job in, and earn a bit of money.'

Even if you have all the raw talent in the world, if it's not nurtured in the right way, and you're not kept on the right path, it's never going to work out. The years from sixteen to eighteen are crucial for your average darts-playing prodigy, when a lot goes on mentally and physically, and a lot can go wrong. The kid leaves school, gets a girlfriend/boyfriend, and as most have already been introduced to alcohol from twelve upwards, it's only natural that many will want to enjoy themselves more and more, and hone their skills less and less.

'Puberty can play a big part in the development of a darts player. It can often get in the way. Guys just want to go out shagging instead of staying in practising their doubles.' Russ Bray doesn't mince his words.

At the time of writing there are four players who dominate the JDC events: Jim Moston, John Brown, Joshua Richardson and Jack Warner.

'There is not really a moment when you decide to turn professional, you sorta start doing better than what you were doing. When you first start you obviously don't do as well as you can. When Devon came over it was a lot harder for him – an eye-opener – than it was for me. When I did it was more of the case if you had the money you could play, but with Devon going to Q-School – everyone who was there was there on merit. It's definitely a tough school. There are no easy games there ...' Joe Cullen pipes up; his prize money so far on the Pro Tour this year is £59,250.

I was relieved to hear that there was now a system in place to support youth talent – hopefully experiences like Jocky Wilson's will be a thing of the past.

'You've got a lot rules these days. I've been involved in darts since 1975, which is a long, long, long time,' Russ Bray told me. 'The kids coming through now have got a better opportunity. If you can cut the mustard then you can make a living. Simple as, whether you are fifty-eight or eighteen. The PDC have created a great youth scheme now, and that's where these boys are coming from. They get to play for a couple of bob as well and nurtured into the next phase of it, the development tour, then challenge, and then you go on the main tour, after you've been to Q-School and get your tour card. And a lot of these youngsters are doing it, and do very well.'

One legend-in-waiting who I find seriously exciting is Beau Greaves, whom I watch playing the Youth World final against Veronica Koroleva from Russia. Beau needed double 5 to take the first leg. The first two darts missed outside and then the third went straight into the centre of the bed. Cool as you like, but then the Russian stepped it up a gear and threw like a darting champ to take the title, after Beau had a bit of a wobble. A few hours later I'm sat in the backstage press room that has had the honour of hosting many showbiz stars. 'We even had the blind black fella here,' Bob Potter told me, as I went to meet Beau in the flesh. I bump into Martin Adams and we get talking about the Youth Final. I mention that Beau should have won.

'Well, she didn't. It's all about them doubles at the end, innit? You see,' is his expert and valid opinion.

Beau Greaves, a thirteen-year-old girl from Doncaster, is the poster girl for the next generation of the BDO players. I had to track her down after both Trina Gulliver and Deta Hedman had waxed lyrical about her darting skills.

As I spent some time with Beau and her dad at Lakeside, it struck me that perhaps Beau didn't know what she was letting herself in for, especially after she played Michael van Gerwen and he said that he 'had less problems with Jamie Caven' than he had playing Beau, and that 'if she keeps playing this well she can join the men's'. That she may be destined to be the woman (when she is a little older) who took on the men and beat them at their own game in their own arena of the PDC.

'I don't come from a sporty family; I started playing darts with my brother and my dad. You think you know where the dart is going to go, but it's all down to how good you think you are.'

'Was van Gerwen as good as you thought he was going to be?'

'I don't know because it was like only the one leg we had, and that was amazing. I'd like to play professionally and I'll probably give the PDC a try. Everybody thinks that men are better than women … but I'm practising every day.'

I will leave you with the image of a thirteen-year-old girl beating a lot of men who all think they are really good at darts. We shall just have to wait five years or so until she is old enough to enter Q-School to see what she's really made of.

CULLEN VS. CADBY

'The young ones don't have that stage as much so it's hard to maintain or understand the pressure that they are under to do it again and again and again. It's fine when they're on the pro tour and you're in the pens, but when you're onstage it's not as easy to do it day after day after day.'

Leon Davis

On the fifth day of the 2017 William Hill World Championship at Alexandra Palace, I watched Corey Cadby obliterate Qiang Sun in three straight sets, at precisely the same time as Barry Hearn was holding a press conference detailing how much money the PDC was pumping into the game and how all the fans were going to be rewarded with a ticket price freeze. A few people in the press room had one eye on Barry and one on the LCD TVs beaming out the live darts from across the way and there was an audible murmur when Corey's average reached 102.4 (the highest ever in a preliminary round) and flashed large on the screen. I was wandering between the two worlds as I had a vested interest in how Corey was doing. I was interviewing him the next day, and after I'd stood there nodding my quiff at Barry, pretending to be engrossed along with the rest of them, I would edge slowly out of the room and then run across the Palm Court into the main arena to watch the action in the flesh. The usual rule is that if a player loses then he bails immediately and there is no interview afterwards in the media room or anywhere else, but the reality was that no player so far had given an in-depth interview win or lose as they 'had their head in the game', to quote Magic Dave.

By the time Barry wrapped up his announcement after a lengthy Q&A there was a new level and kind of energy zapping around the usually sedate press room.

'His average was 102.4.'

'Fuck me. I bet Cullen is practising his doubles.'

This hype worked its way across the Palm Court into the Sky TV announcers' box and infected the first half of the commentary of the game, as we shall hear.

Later that night, after three more games, Corey played Joe Cullen, and everything changed for me and for darts. A game of darts as a cultural moment; the rules of engagement; the direction of this book; and my view of the sport as a modern phenomenon, when it became bigger than it had ever been and on its way to being a global sporting phenomena; the atom split and the box was opened.

The stage was set perfectly for Cullen vs. Cadby. Even though most were saying that this was the start of something big for the Aussie, I was rooting for Joe. He was such a good sport when I was up in his chalet in Minehead, six weeks before; all he wanted to do was to scoff a pan of super pasta cheesy rice noodles whilst it was still warm, and all I wanted was to put him on the record. Plus I've got a soft spot for people from Yorkshire and Joe has a certain twinkle in his eye that will not hinder him becoming a household name and already had me hooked. But that was before I'd spent some time hanging onto the Corey's coat-tails as he is one big lairy Aussie ...

The epic showdown began with the classic cheesy house walk-on tune of 'Freed from Desire' by Gala and 'Wile Out' by Ms Dynamite, each player giving it everything they possibly could, accompanied by the younger, B-team walk-on girls (the established Charlotte and Daniella being rested for the last thirty-two).

It was more like a wrestling match once the two players actually got onto the stage. The girls pouted and posed and John McDonald did his thing and revved the crowd up – this was the last match of the night. By now they were roaring in every sense. Cadby was up there like some bogan with a skew-whiff haircut and started as he meant to go on: giving it everything. He danced across the stage like a stag at his do when they play his favourite song, right up to the jug of water and even wiggled his bum a little bit as he poured out two glasses of water. Giving it the highest of high. The largest of large. Joe Cullen wasn't shy either – he did a bit of a walkabout with a high and low clap and gave Corey a hefty slap on the back before they got down to business, with the crowd still singing along to Cadby's walk-on song. The two men fist-bumped and Corey threw first.

Corey landed the first 180 eight minutes into the match, then Joe missed a double 18 and handed Corey a chance, which he took – after his ritualistic blowing on fingers, cooling them down, perhaps – to win the first set with a bullseye, double top.

Twenty-five minutes in, Joe looked at his mate Devon Petersen, sitting to the right of the stage, and mouthed, *Big leg*. Afterwards I asked what Joe was saying.

'Joe is a talent and really seeing his potential,' Devon confirmed. 'And he won it with a 12 darter after saying that – he knew at that point that he was going to win.'

Corey won the first set after Joe had stormed two games to one ahead, going out on a precise 109 (T19, 12 and then double top). He didn't even bother pulling out his darts, he just turned and walked off the oche to the edge of the stage, punched the air and barked, 'Come on!'

Joe watched this detachedly through hooded eyes, like he'd seen it all before, like it was really unnecessary to be actually stood so near to this annoyance, in front of all these drunken people chanting and singing tunes at one another. In response, he nodded three times and said 'yup' as cool as you like, with a face as stone cold as could be. That was the moment when Joe knew he could take down the big lairy bugger and move on to the next round. He had his head in the right place and his game was progressing deeper and deeper into the zone needed to constantly hone in on those doubles, and Corey was more bothered about giving it the big one in front of the crowd.

Joe kept his concentration and his mind together and this, mixed with his luck holding out, produced some of the finest darts played at the competition, and the greatest darts I will ever see with my own eyes. Each player desperately wanted to win and this pushed both of them to the limits of their ability. Joe played better, hitting almost every double, and after an hour of amazing darts, he won 3–1.

'I think I was burnt. I was throwing really well but he just took crucial pegs and I wasn't unhappy the way I played – I think I played pretty good. It was either his go or my go. I'll break him and he'll break me straight back. I was comfortable, real comfortable mate,' Corey told me afterwards. 'I think the time and the tiredness got to me a bit – preparing for two massive games in the same night – near an hour. Both of us didn't want to lose but at the end of the day there is always one winner and one loser.'

A JOURNEY TO MITCHELLS PLAIN

Now we travel to the Deep South, to my beloved South Africa, and so I have to set this up properly, I have to pay my respects to the land that stole my heart twenty years ago and is now the place I consider my home, culturally and emotionally.

South Africa: the land of the braai, the jol, the red red roads that lead who-knows-where but usually to the bottle stores, the cafés and spazas and bubbie uncle and auntie corner stores and beyond. A beautiful landscape of yellow Victorian houses, Putco buses, vibracrete and razor wire, armed-response garden sheds dotted around the place, glue-sniffing gangs of kids roaming the Southern Suburbs at the crack of dawn, plumes of smoke from roadside braais, religious groups rallying on wastelands around Johannesburg day and night, Sowetan peri-peri chicken shisas, minibus taxis swerving all over the place, buying your way out of trouble, riding high, running low, sound systems in the trunk of your car, amped, I'm amped; raving, I'm raving. We come to party, we come to part ways. I came in tight and went out loose.

I came. I saw. I conquered. I made lank friends and I lost a few along the way. I had a ton of fun and I cried my heart out. I flew so high that I thought I would never be able to come down, and I dipped so, so low I couldn't imagine ever being able to simply walk round the corner to the 7-Eleven for a packet of fags and a pint of milk without having to hold onto something. And that isn't just the drugs talking, or me talking about the drugs, either. I crashed cars, I narrowly escaped death, I rubbed shoulders with some right skollies, who by rights should have spun me over, done me in and perhaps retired on the proceeds. I walked the lonely road through suburbs and dorps and towns so alien to me that I could have been on Mars, but instead of wishing I were elsewhere (which I do a lot of the time when I'm in England), I loved every minute of it. You have to understand how I feel about my adopted home of South Africa, hence this feature-length intro. You have to get what it means to me and why this part of the book is so important.

This is the landscape and culture into which thirty-year-old Devon Petersen was born. Just to the south-east of the Southern Suburbs, lies Mitchells Plain, aka the Cape Flats, home and birthplace of the Spartan.

'My dad played for a team that was from Heideland, near Athlone side, and because it was pre-'94, they got moved to Mitchells Plain, bought a house and stayed there.'[1]

---

[1] This is an important detail that I can't let go by without further explanation. Devon's was one of the thousands of non-white families moved out from totally mixed, integrated areas – such as District 6 – thanks to the insane Apartheid laws (the fuckers wanted all the best areas for whites-only). Whole communities were broken up and dissipated across the dusty, desert-like plain to the south-east of the city, more commonly referred to as the 'Cape Flats', which by the end of the nineties, were a no-go area for most. It was under control of criminal gangs. Gangs who went by names like: The Young Americans, Hard Livings, Nice Time Boys, Mongrels, Scorpions, Laughing Boys. Most gang members like their buttons or tik [Crystal Meth or Ice], guns, customised cars, hip hop and dope. They speak in the most amazing Cape slang accent, a mix between English, Afrikaans and Cape Malay, and are Muslim, descendants from Malaysia. Down there is where you will find the real South African gangsters, and it was an area I was instantly drawn to.

Devon grew up keeping out of trouble and swerving the gangs, listening to American hip hop, eating Gatsbys, playing soccer for local team Liverpool Portland and putting in the hours whilst studying at Mondale high school in Athlone. Darts has always been in his family thanks to his father and uncles, and in South Africa darts is perceived as a coloured sport, in reference to the Apartheid classification of 'coloured'. Black (bottom), Coloured (middle), White (top), which was part of the divide-and-conquer strategy that D. F. Malan's laws of apartheid enforced on the less fortunate people of South Africa.

And one aspect of darts that has persistently struck me is how white it is. I can't help asking Devon about this.

'Because sport is one of the only places where you can cross over – go past the colour barrier. And it's only your talent and performance that count. Being one of the only black players – along with Kyle Anderson [who had his visa refused in 2016, as he applied for a Tier 2 Sports Visa but at the time of writing darts is not officially recognised as a sport] – I find it a bit easier – because we're different, people find it easier to be attracted to us. It's like being given boiled chicken every day and then I just gave you a bit of BBQ chicken – you'd love the BBQ chicken a lot more ...'

'But you must have felt some racism at some point when you came here.'

'Look, you do get – not racism, really – but it's more banter, as they call it. It's an easy target, but I've never ever taken it seriously, and coming from South Africa pre-'94 – it's really not something I deal with, as coming from South Africa where I'm not known as a black player so it's like you're calling me black just because I'm tanned? Your women buy fake tan all the time ... to look like us!'

Devon qualified after the PDC came to South Africa and held the Players World Championship tournaments from 2007 to 2013, and Devon won three. He began to see that he was picking up some momentum and form. He'd just made the South African team, and plucked up the courage to tell his dad that he was going to quit his banking job and go over to the UK to play there. 'Everybody thought it was just something you'd say. No one believed me.'

And after throwing this statement down, Devon won all the major trophies in South Africa and Africa, won the qualifier, flew over to London and played in his first World Championship, and promptly lost to Jamie Caven, which must have hurt like hell but was a necessary part of his darting development.

Everyone I spoke to, when I mentioned that I'd been hanging out with Devon, had one thing to say: What a guy, a star in the making. And this was beside his skill as a darts player. The fact that he has beaten Michael van Gerwen 6–1 ('he has what Taylor has over players, you feel like you have to play your very best all the time, as you know that van Gerwen can turn at any time – but now he is showing signs of being beatable') shows that he has both the skills and the personality to go far. And with darts it's all about the person. Okay, so you've gotta be able to play but can you tell the difference between James Wade and Adrian Lewis? These podgy white men all look and play the same to me, and Devon is one of the most loved and popular darts players because of everything he isn't.

'Some people recognise you all the time, especially at darts events. It's funny for me because I'm from Mitchells Plain, I'm a *boijki* from a disadvantaged community and people are asking for autographs, wanting photos and T-shirts. It's still very, very surreal for me. It's really crazy. A different world.'

After his first appearance at Ally Pally, Devon attended the first-ever Q-School and won his tour card on the second day, which meant his adventure in darts could begin for real.

'We met through my sponsor,' remembered Joe Cullen, PDC player on the rise. 'At the time he was really interested in Devon and we went to check him out and there was an instant liking – we just got along immediately. He came to live with me, never paid any rent ... No, it's common knowledge in the darts world that we're brilliant friends.

Playing darts with your best friend, doing what you love with your best friend, there is not much more you can ask for …'

Devon moved his life to England – no small thing in itself – and initially stayed with his ex-pat friends in London, which eased him in, before he ventured out, travelling up north because of his friendship with Joe.

'It was different at first. Especially when you go up north. When I used to come over I would stay in London and that was kinda multi-cultural, and everybody was an individual basically, but when you go up north you can see that I would stick out like a sore thumb, and obviously the accent didn't help.'

'So you felt the sting of a cold English reality?'

'Ja, sometimes you get those knobheads. You can just see that they still got that racism in them but they can't let it out because they know it's taboo.'

Devon came to the World's a day before he was scheduled to play and knew no one. He met Joe. 'I saw this kid rush through as he was about to go onstage and we caught each other's eyes. I wished him well and that was it … We never thought that moment was the start of our brotherhood.' The two met up again at Q-School and thanks to Devon's openness at their initial meeting, they ended up with the same management and rooming together on the European tour.

This is one of the features of darts that makes it so special. Why should such a seemingly mundane, repetitive sport (that is often dismissed as a working-class boozy pastime) refuse to go quietly and sink back into obscurity just like skittles or Morris dancing or archery? Why the fuck has it stuck around and refused to die?

'I think it's the individuality of the sport itself. It gives a lot of people the chance to be a player. A fat guy can't become a football player, but its appeal is that you're seeing normal guys – Jay Wilson or Steve Brown, for instance – it's almost like you're seeing a fan on the stage …' And here Devon returns to one of the cornerstones of darts. Its immense popularity is down to the fact that you can't clean up the sport and your players are a mirror of the fans in the stands of the exhibition centres, holiday camps and technology-sponsored arenas. It's the fans that make the sport what it is.

'What are the fans like? Is there such a thing as darts groupies?'

'I think if you're talking male and female, the sport has become more diverse, there are not groupies coming in here lying naked ...' Devon told me.

'It's only ever happened twice!' Joe Cullen shouted from the other side of the room of the chalet in Minehead. The darts weekenders I witnessed seemed like a lot was packed into a short space of time, and I put this to Devon – that a full weekend of darts is a wild ride indeed, even for a Spartan from the Cape Flats.

'Because it's an event that only happens once a year and the tickets sell out very quickly, so you're not sure when you will get back here. It's one of the craziest because it's at Butlin's, and when you are playing you are amongst the fans all the time – going to the shop, going out to eat or drinking in the pubs – it's here where you interact most with the fans. When you're playing at the World Champs, you're cordoned off in the VIP backstage and when you're done you're straight back to the hotel.'

Drinking and drugs play a huge role in the cultural history of the UK, and there is no denying that a lot of darts fans like to get really wasted. I've seen it. I've done it. I'm doing it right now ... And like it or not it's a vital part of the whole PDC experience [disclaimer: the PDC strictly forbids the use of any illegal substances at any of its events], but can it effect or enhance your game?

'I think because it's such a precision game, if you were to go onstage stone cold sober it would be a daunting task because you've got the crowd behind you, you've got the adrenalin pumping and the margins are so small that if you miss a dart that could be the difference of £10,000 or £350,000, which is a massive thing,' Devon reckoned.

'But it's all about the booze?' I had to slay the elephant in the room.

'Drinking doesn't play that big of a part any more, not like it did back in the day when it was all about drinks. You've got the DRA and the Olympic drug committee watching and players get tested and so it's a massively controlled environment.'

Which may sound a bit like Devon toeing the PDC corporate line, but having got to know him and spend some quality hang time, I know that he really believes this. And when you look at the money side of things, he does have a point. There is a lot riding on your arrows these days. Which leads me to the other train of thought I've been (stupidly) chasing throughout this adventure. Darts and drugs. Are they an oxymoron?

'I've never ever seen any drugs.' Devon is adamant. 'Because we have the testing, so with drugs there is too much on the line. I've never seen any fans doing anything bad like that. You can't class them as darts fans individually, because they are watching darts and you're doing drugs. The one concession they do make is that you can drink but you can't take enhancements ...'

Devon Petersen is a champion in more ways than meets the eye.

THE NATURAL

'A lot of people don't understand. They ask for tips but I've never had to ask for tips. That's just how I am, you're just good at it or you're not.'
Corey Cadby, taking no prisoners

Cut back to a warm (is there any other kind in Australia?) barmy night –19 January 2016 – at the Melton Darts Club, a blue and yellow striped low-level industrial-looking darts and bingo club studded with air-con units like piercings on a Goth, just next to the Botanical Gardens and the shoddy sports centre on the outskirts of Melton, 20 miles west of Melbourne. A hefty kid with a crazy bogun haircut like a dip-dyed cockatoo gone wrong rumbled up to the oche and over the next few minutes threw a perfect nine-darter. The place went fucking mental and almost ripped itself apart. In the thirty-odd years the club had been going, no one had ever achieved this. Until that moment.

Welcome to the rollercoaster ride of a life that nonchalantly belongs to Corey Cadby, darting genius and next-level superstar. He has kindly let me sit next to him for a short while as he tears across the world with a tattoo on his neck of a crown and the word 'King' underneath, something that I can relate to.

Born in Tasmania but raised in the outer suburb of Westmelton, Corey is the son of Fred Cadby, once the number two player in Australia who used to tour with Simon Whitlock (the guy who now sports a very heavy-metal-like beard and is ranked 16th in the world) and so his move into the world of darts was almost inevitable.

'I've always thrown a dart but I wasn't allowed to play in a competition until I could count and chalk, when I was sixteen,' Corey tells me. His first darting memory is waking his dad up at five in the morning to spread the good word about the bullseye he had just hit. 'I can't remember what he said, but the name stuck!' Corey has been known ever since as 'Bullseye! Bullseye!'

The first time I heard Corey's name was back in the Crazy Horse Room that was doubling as both the press room and players' warm-up bar/lounge at Butlin's Minehead, when I was grilling referee Russ Bray like George Foreman about the next stars of the game. I needed bringing up to speed since I was still so clueless. Corey had literally just won the PDC Unicorn World Youth Championship final, taking home a hefty £10,000 prize – his first ever game in England. After that all eyes were most definitely on him.

'I was really sick with a bad cold. I couldn't even get out of bed. And then four hours before the game I had to get up and get ready. I was as crook as a dog so I drank a lot and it sweated right out of me ...' Corey remembered, after I asked him what he thought of the English institution of Butlin's holiday camp, which was not a lot.

After his nine-darter, Corey has had an unbelievably effortless rise from there (Westmelton) to here (Alexandra Palace). He never had any hopes or expectations of coming to England, of playing at Ally Pally and making a huge entrance into the darts world. It just happened, and the most insane element to all of this is that the darts pretty much go where Corey wants them to, like a diviner, following the dowsing rods.

'It's just natural. You can either be good at a sport or not. Honestly I have no idea. They say practice makes perfect, but to be honest I don't really practise. I don't like to say so because no one believes me, but I honestly, really, don't.' And these words sound so natural to him, not like he's boasting or anything. Just telling it like it is.

Corey's journey into darts may sound like it was inevitable as we wander around the inner workings of Alexandra Palace, but darts really isn't on the same scale down under. Yeah, Corey plays with his mates in the pub and there is growing interest in the game, but darts is not an aspiration. It's certainly not a common route to fame. 'Back home darts is pretty big, but when you come over here, this is just huge, mate. I just wish darts over here was based in Australia. That would make things a helluva lot easier,' Corey said, referencing the twenty-four-hour nightmare of a commute.

He's just twenty-one and has only been playing for five years since he learnt how to count, but there's no doubt the skills are there in abundance.

'Did you always want to play here?'

'I've never thought of England, to be honest; I never thought I'd get this far. But like I said, my life has changed completely with that nine-darter ...'

The road may have been swift, but it certainly wasn't smooth. Corey's brother died in a heartbreaking car accident when he was twelve and this had a profound effect on him. He never really got over it and the grief manifested itself in some wild-as-fuck behaviour. Our talk turned to the struggles that a lot of sixteen-year-old players have when they have to make a choice between the darts and going out getting wasted and chasing girls with their mates.

'Ah, mate, I've had the ... I've lived my life already ...' His sentence trailed off as a recollection of a truly chaotic time flashes into his mind. Dealing with grief for the first time is traumatic for anyone. When that person is your brother, and you're in a formative period of development yourself, well that can compound the trauma. The temptation to self-destruct can crawl from the shadows and present an appealing escape; the only escape.

'So with your brother dying and you getting annihilated ...'

'It's just the way I dealt with it. But about ten months ago I actually started going and talking about my brother's death to a professional. I'd never ever done that, never had the chance because I thought I wouldn't need to. You gotta speak what you think otherwise it's just going to mumble on yer mind and ... darts is a massive head sport. Like a head game. You got something on your mind you're not going to play the darts that you want. No way.'

Corey ended up in prison, along with two other brothers. 'We were running amuck and just doing stupid shit, mate, that I wouldn't do sober ... We were all in the slammer at the same time as well. So it was good for back-up ...' And this is where the story takes us back to darts.

Corey and his brothers used to go out and about acquiring goods that were easy to sell, and always had the option to cash in their haul at Cash Converters, who sponsored his first big UK tournament – the Minehead Cash Converters Players Championship, a fact that I find ironic.

Corey has a sponsor called Harrows (who manufacture darts) at the moment but they 'will be going down the road because I've had these massive offers ...' Which means we will be hearing and seeing a lot more of Corey in the next year or so.

Corey's story is a bit of a rarity in the darting world, not just because of his honesty and openness about his difficult youth, but because he is from the next generation of players who haven't come out of the pub and so alcoholism isn't the only demon they will have to watch out for. Talking to Corey also makes me wonder how many players are addicted to gambling – another industry closely involved in darts sponsorship.

But it was the love of a woman that ultimately saved Corey from self-destruction and from any more time locked up.

And, as they say, the rest is history, especially after Corey beat Phil Taylor in the first round of the Perth Masters. 'To beat Phil Taylor was a dream come true. He was the legend who made darts itself. To beat him on television was incredible. But to accomplish that is something that will always be the best thing to happen so early in my career, and for him to speak to me after the game, the words that he said, has given me more confidence.'

Corey Cadby is probably one of the most talented and charismatic players I will ever get to hang out with, and the reason he opened up to me was because I was honest and open about my own history, which is a by-product of the abundance and appetite of the drug culture in the UK. The next generation of players will have a totally different set of demons to hold at bay, and this is something that their management and the PDC will have to be aware of.

Interlude #7 – Sending Cliff Richard over the moon

I'm back in the UK for the build-up to the William Hill World Darts Championship and the BDO Lakeside World Professional Championship, and just as I'm about to take my darts back to Flight Club (in desperation, I may add) for a serious bit of practising, I discover this great website called Capital Arrows that maps out the pubs of London where you can play darts.

I spend a bit of time on the site and having scrutinised the Soho section, I grab my darts and jump on the 'dilly. There are three pubs in Soho that still have a board and today I am going to play in them all.

Wandering down Berwick Street takes me back to when I was thirteen, when me and my mates would pile onto the Green Line coach in the middle of St Albans and get dropped off in walking distance to the West End. Our mission was to roam through Soho, checking out the sex shops and other seedy goings-on, and if we were feeling extra rude we'd dive into a peep show, which I always found pretty traumatic. Thirty-odd years on I have a set of darts in my hand and I'm back with a very different purpose.

As I cut through the Berwick Street market, it's obvious that street food is pretty much keeping this once-iconic market alive, and struggling through the queue snaking out of the fish & chip shop, it occurs to me that the only real soul left in Soho is the food and the pubs. Everything else has deserted, even the few remaining sex shops look like they are from another era, out of time and place.

The ten or so food stalls that make up the market are serving up the odd meal to the usual Soho types: pizza to office girls, Jerusalem falafel to queens and stylists, Vietnamese to heavy Ray-Ban frames and ginger sideburns and Victorian beards as found on every UXP designer this side of Beirut. The one massive loss is that the legend of Daddy Kool is no longer, and the entrance that used to lead me downstairs into the basement mecca for all things reggae is just another shop selling vintage clothes. I worshipped that place; it was the greatest place in the West End to dig out Greensleeves 12". The sign used to read: 'Daddy Kool is open in the basement. Reggae – Studio 1 – Roots – Ska' and down I'd trek …

The first pub is the Red Lion in Kingly Street, which, according to Capital Arrows, is 'the most dangerous darts pub in London', which makes it first on my list.

With a pint in hand I start to practise my game. The darts still refuse to go where I want and after becoming so frustrated with trying to hit the twenty I begin a game of round the clock and it takes a fucking age to move on to the '2' and then for some reason I try with my left eye closed and suddenly I'm hitting the right number every time. This is a major breakthrough. I can't quite believe that it's happening. It must be a run of flukes. But then I get to 18 and I keep going. Before I know it I've hit the twenty and I'm out. I open my eye to check that I'm really out – which I am, this is a miracle. I retrieve my darts and head for the next pub.

The Glasshouse Stores in Brewer Street is next, and on my way I pass the front door of what used to be Bermuda Shorts, the first production house to rep me as a director, for whom I made a music video for Sir Cliff Richard. I'm not kidding. This isn't some kind of gonzo trip. This is the truth. This is history.

After finding that none of their regular directors wanted to make a video for Cliff, they approached me. I threw a few thoughts together, recycled some others, and pitched the idea of Cliff flying through a very kitsch digital landscape like a fairy, singing his little heart out and (literally) hanging tough. He liked the idea. So I got to drive down to his humongous yard in Weybridge with the guy who ran the record company that was releasing the single – and paying for the video. It took twenty minutes to get to Cliff's pad after going through the security gate. By this time, I was dying for the toilet and had to nip off upon arrival and it was here, as I was sat there in Sir Cliff Richard's downstairs toilet, that I noticed it was full of awards – as you do. I picked one up – TV Times Award 1980 for Most Exciting Singer on TV – and I realised that I had actually watched the show when I was a kid. Fuck me. From there to here and now I'm sat on the king's throne taking a much-needed pony.

I washed my hands and followed the noise and my first sight of Sir Cliff was this little man in a khaki jumpsuit running around his massive kitchen making tea for everyone – by now there was quite an entourage: his sisters, their husbands, the video commissioner, the producer, Cliff's manager, the record company MD. He spotted me and jogged over. Might as well have been a cartwheel.

'Hi, I'm Cliff!' He was so fucking energetic.

'Adz. Great to meet you.' We shook hands, then –

'I'm really happy to be working with you! I love your work!' I thought he was taking the piss, so I laughed and said, "Right, me too." The penny dropped. I realised that he wasn't joking. Cliff wasn't big on laughs. We had tea and I talked him through the video and he was happy as Larry.

I shot the video – big blue screen for Cliff to fly about – and then spent six weeks with a team of animators compositing it on Macs in an attic in Soho overlooking Brewer Street, constantly fighting with the producers about how to make the fucking thing. The last few days of production were a bit manic and it all ended up in a fancy-schmancy post facility in Frith or Dean or Greek Street, putting the final sparkle to the video (which was going out the next night on an ITV chat show – Frank Skinner introduced it as 'it looks like The Matrix' – just imagine, Sir Cliff Richard as Neo!). The video went out and Cliff was over the moon with it. The next morning when I went in to the office the MD told me to pack my stuff and get the fuck out of there, as apparently I was too much of a liability. There was a lesson to be learnt somewhere in there …

Glasshouse. Darts. One eye closed. Much better. I play with a guy who plays for a bank team in Clerkenwell who can certainly play. I have a pint of something very random (it's a Sam Smith's pub) and a chat, during which he tells me a tale from the Jersey Open that I can't repeat verbatim for legal reasons, but the one thing I can feed back is thanks to the rather large amount of money the average BDO player spends on booze at tournaments, s/he has to have a pretty decent job the rest of the time to be able to cover not just the constant travel and accommodation expenses, but also the relentless boozing. The prize money isn't going to cover that unless you are Glen Durrant (2017 BDO World Champion, prize money £100,000), and this makes me think of the BDO a little differently. I pull my darts out of the board and bid my financial friend goodbye and head off for the last stop on my darting tour of Soho. As I get outside it's pissing with rain. A perfect day for darts, then.

The last pub on my mini-tour is the Comedy in Oxenden Street (which is not strictly Soho but is still the West End), a massive place that to quote the website is 'Famous for its stand-up comedy and attracting top names such as Jimmy Carr and Ricky Gervais. If stand-up comedy is not your thing, rest easy, we have a lot more to offer ...' I wander about, looking for the board for a while, before the nice Croatian lady behind the bar directs me to the first floor (first of many), which turns out to be a pretty barren place, and a direct contrast to Flight Club. This is the other end of darts, the neglected and uncommercial and tucked-away upstairs. I reckon this floor will soon become one of those all-you-can-eat world buffets or filled with table tennis or foosball tables in some better-late-than-never attempt to woo in the hipster crowd. I force myself to throw some darts, which, even with one eye closed, fail to go anywhere near where I want them to, and after I've done my pint of shandy, I tramp downstairs with a bit of a headache and out into the drizzling afternoon with my beer buzz fading fast and the thought of fighting the commuters really not helping at all.

There is something comfortingly nostalgic about playing darts in Soho. After spending an hour in the Chinese supermarket in Chinatown, overloading on char sui buns, Kikkomans and other spicy treats, I'm on my way back to the tube, passing the corner where the notorious venue known simply as the 'Dive Bar' used to be, underneath the Kings Head, which is now just another Chinese restaurant. The place was always full of art students (I was one) and Sloanes, proto-Yardies, and the weird and the wonderful. A bit of a warm-up for the Mud Club really, but that is another story. It was always rammed and smoky and the funk hammered the eyes, ears and nose. The food may be better in Soho now, but back then the culture was something else, and there was probably a lot more darting action to be found. Whatever was going down it was real and not just media-subsumed. It was all we had. It was brilliant and completely crap at the same time, but that was all we knew.

CHAPTER EIGHT

CONTINENTAL DARTS

'I love the game. I love to play, actually, I don't really like watching, but I love to play.'

Michael van Gerwen

The Germans and the Dutch are darting mad and I hit the Continent to see just how big it is out there. I spend some time with one player from each country. As we all know by now, the latest superstar of darts is Michael van Gerwen, who hails from the Low Countries, and then there's Max Hopp, superstar-in-waiting from Germany – 22-years-old, good-looking, tall, no beer belly (yet), ranked 45 in the world. He's an outsider in the UK but already a huge star in Germany, even though his skills are not yet honed, which creates an interesting dichotomy, a massive national fan base, but he can't (yet) bring home the wins.

ROTTERDAM

'Amazingly Germany is our biggest growth area. Thirteen per cent of the tickets to the World Darts Championship were sold to Germany. That is unbelievable, as there were only 4 per cent to Holland. Germany is a massive market. They're taking the trouble to come over, pay for hotels, flights, fuck me. This game has the ability to transcend things like golf, because there are so little restrictions and it's so much more mass-market.'

Barry Hearn

The indicator that darts was beginning to reach a sporting critical mass outside of the UK came after it was announced that the PDC Premier League final was to be staged in Rotterdam's Ahoy Arena on 28 May 2016, and it sold out in a matter of minutes – 12,000 tickets sold out in nine minutes, to be precise.

After this there was a serious amount of media build-up to the event both in the Netherlands and the UK, which helped push the sport into areas it had never existed in before. Gladwell would call it the tipping point but I would call it about fucking time.

'I went to Rotterdam for the Premier League last year – and you will hear those words bandied around a lot – "Rotterdam and the Premier League" – because those who were there – and I was included – have never been to a show like it, ever,' John McDonald, the Rebel MC, told me from somewhere behind the scene of a big PDC event. 'If you were judged on that show alone for the rest of your career, you are forever in an all-star line-up. It was magnificent. The reaction. The crowd. The atmosphere. It was like a performance from one of the gods of rock. You went out on that stage and the roar and the cheering – 12,000 voices. It made the hairs on the back of your neck stand up, and I've worked 80,000 people in Wembley. I've done the Ryder Cup, 45,000 people live with 300 million viewers around the world, and nothing could get you up like that – to walk on the stage and go, "Good evening, Rotterdam! Bang!!!" Barry saw that all those years ago and knew that it was going to work. He knew that's how it would be and we were all like, "Come on, it's 500 people in a town hall somewhere, it's never gonna be …" The Premier League is all arenas.' The biggest venues we go to we sell out. Darts has come so far from its original place it's nearly unrecognisable.'

The Dutch Prime Minister (who will later call up and interrupt my interview with MvG to congratulate him) had asked the fans to wear orange. The press in each country hyped the shit out of their respective players. The Power vs. Mighty Mike. The greatest player ever meets his nemesis. Big time Battle Royale.

'I'm proud of England, and I will show you who the greatest is …' The Power had boasted on the pre-roll tape on Sky, and consequently there was an arena's worth of booing as he walked out to Snap's 'The Power' – which is still quite a belter when it drops. The rah-rah dancing girls onstage were shaking their thing as Phil wobbled his way down the runway flanked by a Dutch walk-on girl dressed like a *Thunderbirds* pilot, all enhancements bouncing to the Eurobeat, as the surgeon intended.

Then it was Mike's turn. His girl was dressed in a lime-green mini-dress and fat gold rope chain (subconsciously channelling Run DMC), which wasn't the only plastic on show. Neither walk-on girls I recognise. They must be the continental ones.

'It's my country, my fans, my people. I wear green but I'm flying an orange flag,' MvG laid down. 'I will show who is the world's number one!' Which he did, and swiftly beat The Power 7 legs to 5, after a 50 finish on 18, double 16. Pity he didn't actually wear an orange shirt (the only possible reason for this is that van Gerwen is locked deeply into his brand of lime green and is scared that perhaps no one will recognise him in any other colour. I've only seen him in anything else on one occasion), as this would have distilled the moment in the collective memories of his home fans for ever. The fact that he won on home ground was momentous, but not entirely unexpected as it was slap bang in the middle of twenty-six wins in the 2016 season.

THE MAXIMISER

'I used to be the kind of person when I lose it would be the end of the world. I used to cry for nearly an hour. I used to be very upset with myself – which is the wrong way to be after you lose. You need to accept it because the only person you can blame is yourself – you lost because you didn't perform well. There is no other reason. You didn't perform.'

Max Hopp, star in waiting

The place is rammed with Germans singing 'Das Lied der Deutschen' and a flag with a lot of red, gold and black is flapping boisterously about over some rather questionable costumes – from German naval officers looking like ropey Richard Geres to some lad dressed as an old-school raver wearing, quite randomly, a Luftwaffe flying cap who I bump into coming back from the bar, to the standard, yet horrendous car crash of a shell suit topped off with a blond mullet wig, which I was initially introduced to by the third Austrian football team and since then I can't help noticing a lot of that particular look. Tonight – for one night only – Alexandra Palace has turned into a proper beer keller, because of one young lad.

'I'm a really, really young player from Germany but I'm really, really experienced. I'm the highest achiever in Germany reaching the World Championship at the age of twenty. There are a lot of people in the media who are pushing my age and that can affect my game sometimes and I have problems handling it to be honest. Because it's very, very mental ...'

Max Hopp's rise towards superstardom happened in the blink of an eye in his home country after he won the boys' title of the 2011 WDF World Cup, and tonight, when he enters the arena smiling proudly underneath his hair gel with his diamond stud earring refracting the light, he carries the weight of the whole of the German dart-loving public on his sprightly shoulders. There isn't anyone else they can look to as he has travelled the furthest, is the most awarded, with the highest average. Max is the one, and as he is only just out of his teenage years it must be scary stuff indeed.

Leading up to his entrance tonight [at the 2017 World's] I have been asking everyone I meet (and anyone who will listen) what they think about Max and they all say the same thing: Too much pressure. He's good, but they are expecting way too much too soon. Leave the kid alone and let him get on with it at his own pace.

'My first memory of darts was the [2008] World Championship final between Kirk Shepherd and John Part, and afterwards I started to play and enjoy darts and then I came to the Ally Pally at sixteen – the second youngest player ever to do that.' The youngest player to ever qualify for the World's is the superbly named Mitchell Clegg, who was sixteen years and thirty-seven days old when he played in the 2007 World's.

If I say here it's not just about the winning you will know that Max has lost a fair few games at world-class level, but he's still turning heads. The first time I get to see him play in the flesh he beats Martin Wolfie Adams in a cross-organisation challenge, which Wolfie gurns, grimaces and whistles through, essentially hamming up each miss like an animated old-school naughty seaside postcard, and even pulling down the very unlucky score of 26 at one point, known colloquially as Bed and Breakfast. But it's televised and it's a win for the Maximiser. Apparently, it's all about the TV exposure, as Keith Talent testified in Martin Amis's *London Fields*:

> Expedient to a fault in most things, Keith was a confessed romantic when it came to his darts ... The deal went something like this. A house in Twickenham or thereabouts: in the environs of Twickenham. An aviary. Park the wife and kid. Keep greyhounds. A household name. Figure in the England manager's plans: throw your heart out in an England shirt. An ambassador for the sport, a credit to the game. Give every barmaid in Britain one: no female pub goer on earth can resist a celebrity darter, a personality. Tours of Scandinavia, Australia, Canada, the States. Build up a personal library of every victory on video. Be on television, a face known by millions. On TV innit. TV. TV ...

*

As I've watched Max battle – both on and off TV – a series of world-class players (including van Gerwen, the juggernautical magic monster who he lost to in just over twelve minutes), I've noticed that when he's under pressure (every time he plays) his cheeks go red and he blinks heavily as if to stop the tears from even thinking about showing on his face. It's an honest emotional hook, and I'm instantly drawn in and become his biggest fan. Before I know it I'm rooting for lightie Max to slay the giants he so bravely takes on. It must be an absolute nightmare and a total mind-fuck to have to square up to the best of the best of the best when you're pretty much starting out and your entire country is basically telling you to win for them or else. That is a clinical definition of pressure, which must be compounded when getting thrashed by the legends of the moment.

'It bothers me a lot,' he told me.

Max pops up on the jumbotron in what first appears to be a motivational video ('Everybody wants to perform on that big stage because all eyes are on you. You are the player and the whole world is watching you so you want to do well, you want to show the world what you are capable of …'), but after actually spending some time with him I realise that's just how earnest and honestly German he really is. He is one of the virgins Phil Taylor was talking about at the start of my darting adventure backstage at Wolverhampton Civic Hall: 'If they haven't come out of the pub, they're the ones who are going to come through without any fear. They've not been poisoned by society, they're virgins as such and they're gonna come out and try their best without any distractions. They haven't had all this shit off people. Once they hit the stage they're gonna get it and it's going to be a massive shock. They're going to come out of their bedrooms or front rooms – they're gonna practise, then they will qualify cos it's quiet where we qualify, then they're gonna come onstage and it's like "holy shit!" and then they will hit the fan then.'

I watch him lose straight sets to Kim Huybrechts and I leave the place and drive home, assuming that he won't be giving an interview, as custom dictates. He should now be in hiding. Magic Dave texts me to say that he has got Max in a corner for me exclusively. Fuck! I make some bullshit excuse that I had to move the car and make it back to Ally Pally in ten mins flat to catch the end of his general press conference with both German and English press.

The other hacks file out and I sit down with Max and his girlfriend's son on a bench in the Palm Court and put him on the record. I ask him to define the darting culture in his homeland.

'The culture of darts in Germany is based around the soft-tip darts. Germans like to gamble as well and they don't like to calculate – it got bigger with the TV events, to be honest. It took some time but now it's very, very big. There are some events that compare to the Alexandra Palace, which attract 3,000 people.'

'But did it grow out of pub culture?'

'We've got British (chips and cider), Irish (Guinness) and German (pretzel and sausage) pubs, but all with a dartboard, so I guess it may have.'

Max was born and raised in Frankfurt and grew up listening to Eminem and Linkin Park but recently moved to a small East German town outside of Nuremberg, where he has a very strict routine.

'I always practise four hours a day. I stick to my routines,' he says defiantly.

I mention that in the UK, darts is seen as a working-class sport and the media and sponsors are somewhat snobbish.

'Really?' Max is genuinely surprised at my statement. 'In Germany darts is growing and it's already bigger than handball, basketball and ice hockey. It's close to being the most viewed sport after football, so German sponsors are coming from every area; it doesn't matter whether it's a bank or a supermarket – they all are interested in the sport.'

This is a revelation to me. One reason could be that the German brand manager doesn't have the old-school imagery lodged back in the bad-old-days of darts. This leads me to start banging on about how the older players still drink a lot whilst they are playing. Max now seems genuinely confused, his brain almost short-circuits at the thought of this. Max doesn't drink when he plays darts, and perhaps he doesn't expect anyone else to? The cynic within me suggests that as he plays them all the time he must just be toeing the PDC party line.

'I know in the eighties the players would drink and smoke onstage but that is many years ago. The PDC is professional for many years now. We don't drink. We play our game. We're always focused, that's how it is and that is what makes this sport now professional. In the eighties and nineties they used to smoke and drink onstage but the PDC stopped that. No alcohol, no cigarettes, just playing darts and that's how we do it and we are so successful with it and it's all a part of the mental game – be fit in your mind and you're going to win.'

'A common problem with boys as darts players is that when they get to sixteen they want to chase girls and drink with their mates. How did you cope with this?' I ask Max.

'Really?' he answers, once again frankly surprised by what I'm telling him. 'I never once lost focus. I have been with my girlfriend for two and half years. Before that I had some relationships as well. I always said that darts started out as my hobby but at a certain point it became my job, and always the first focus is on family and then comes darts – I would never let fun affect my game. To go out with some friends is maybe nice. You always need to be aware that you are in a position playing proper darts, you're a good player. Don't ruin that by going out and having fun for silly things. If you have had a successful year and you have some free time then you can go out and do whatever you want. Work is work and fun is privacy time. Always separate.'

Then talk turns to growing up in the public eye and Max goes a bit quiet. I've obviously struck a nerve. I wonder how it must be when you are the only hope, but also you are still learning to lose, trying to break through from being a decent darts player to being a brilliant world-class one.

'You go into the street with your family and people want pictures – and that's a good thing – but it also can affect your game when you go to a tournament and everybody is watching you and you don't know if you can be yourself.' And this is a true revelation from Max. How can you be your true self when you still are trying to discover who that is?

A few days later at the [World's] semi-final I'm stood next to a German TV producer/presenter and ask him his 'professional' thoughts about Max.

'He is the only one we have, and one day he will be okay,' he tells me.

'Okay? It's too early to tell …' I counter, feeling a lot more loyal to Max than his countryman.

'*Ja*. He is never going to be a greatest player ever. You can tell,' he says with no emotion. No malice. No loyalty. I desperately hope Max proves them all wrong.

The lights drop and the fireworks begin and we are both distracted from our conversation by the spectacle. Fuck me, I think, give the lad a chance.

THE MVG STORY

'You do not know in advance what you have. You only know that you have curiosity. So until you get beyond that mere level of interest, unfulfilled, you don't know what you have or what your story is. Sometimes you get their cooperation and, lo and behold, you find that you don't want it.'

Gay Talese, talking about whether it's easier to write about someone who wants to cooperate or someone who doesn't, as I take it back, once again, to *Frank Sinatra Has a Cold* – the story of when he was assigned to interview the singer, who – it turned out – refused to talk

*

Michael van Gerwen didn't have a cold, he had the hump.

He had laid down his darting philosophy in the straight-to-DVD doc *House of the Flying Arrows*: 'I've got a big passion for darts. It's just myself. I don't do that to entertain them. It's my own game. I just make sure my leg is straight and it's one natural throw, I always play the same. I don't aim. I'm not an aimer, I throw my darts on instinct – they go in or not.'

That may sound like a big claim, but I have watched him play up close and personal; I have witnessed first-hand the moment when, despite increasing noise from the drunken crowd (van Gerwen is never, ever, first on) and the music, something clicked deep within him and the Dutch legend (who was playing reasonably well) switched on his darts guidance system and then let some serious arrows fly – resulting in every fucking dart going exactly where it was intended. And seeing as I was trying to get my own game up, I bow down to the darting skills of Michael van Gerwen.

'Mike's a lovely bloke, you know, he really is ...' says Charlotte Wood, walk-on girl. 'They all react the same when they lose – if you speak to any security you'll hear it's like having a child – they've thrown their dummy out of the pram, but it does mean everything to them and so you can see why they get like that ...'

I first came face to face with Michael in the exotic press room of the Wolverhampton Civic Hall and he looked straight through me as he had sent advance word that he wasn't going to do interviews because he wanted to 'keep his head in the darts', which turned out to be a smoke screen – he just didn't want to talk for a book that he wasn't going to share in the profits. When we meet again he has just won the 2017 William Hill World Championship for the second time, at the end of his most productive and heroic year, during which he won twenty-six titles and over £1.8million, but I am still partially invisible as he only really wants to talk to the 'serious' newspaper reporters and there I am dressed like Captain Haddock. I never claimed to be a reporter. Just a gonzo writer from the back of beyond, which gives us something in common.

Little Michael grew up in a small Dutch town few have ever heard of called Boxtel, famous for some battle or other back in the day when things like that mattered, but little else. It must have been a vacuum of middle-class millennial liberalism even with the castle in the middle of the lake to sneak up on in the middle of the night with your mates and pretend you're going to storm it. He discovered hair gel and darts at roughly the same time – aged thirteen – but Michael is a glorious example of someone who was born to throw an arrow. After giving up on the football (every suburban kid plays dreaming of winning the European Cup) and realising that it was darts he was lekker at, he would have spent his time practising to the sounds of Mad'House and Brainpower whilst fantasising about being able to leave his hometown and see the world via darting global domination. Right from the start, the darts pretty much always went where he threw them.

'It's family. It's human. It's a gift. It's definitely a gift,' said Olly Croft, OBE. 'I remember van Gerwen when he was sixteen, seventeen – he just had the gift of doing it, you know. I watched him play and he just played darts. Just flick, flick, flick. Just natural. Eric and Jocky had to really work to make things happen ...'

Michael practised hard and played his best and worked his way up the Dutch youth rankings and reached the final of the Primus Youth Masters aged fourteen in 2003. Following this he won the German, Norwegian, Northern Irish, Swedish and the Dutch Youth championships, whilst still working as a roof tiler. He found himself playing and ranked third in the BDO before he had turned eighteen.

'I'm a fair guy,' he says. 'I hate people that lie. I speak about my darts, I'm a confident man, and you need to have that confidence. But people sometimes don't like that I'm quite a good dart player.'

By 2006 Michael faced Martin Adams in the final of the Bavaria World Darts Trophy and even though he managed a 170 checkout, lost the title. Perhaps his nerves got the better of him, but a few months later he was presented with an opportunity for revenge after reaching the finals of the Winmau World Masters, again playing Martin. It was a close game but Michael won 7–5 to take the world record as the youngest player ever to take the Masters title at seventeen years and 174 days, a truly remarkable achievement.

After the match Michael went on Dutch TV and told the world that he considered Wolfie a bit of a joke, according to a darts journalist from the Low Countries who filled me in about his journey.

'One or two players say some silly things, things people consider disrespectful, but that's fine as I just put it down to youthful exuberance.' Martin Adams lets off Michael van Gerwen for coating him something chronic on live TV. 'He's young, he's not worldly wise. He's just said a couple of silly things. I've got broad enough shoulders to take it ...'

And it was after that win that Michael made the decision to move to the PDC, something that he must have regretted for a while, when nothing went his way and he began to get his ass handed to him. Playing in the PDC is a completely different experience. It's darts squared, 24/7, and then some. You have to bring your A-game both mentally and physically each and every time you step out in front of the boozy, braying crowd. There is never any slack; never any forgiveness tucked away for those tragic moments when you drop a bollock.

The other problem is that the BDO doesn't prepare you for the other side of darts: the real world where you eventually end up if you are any good. After journeying across the chasm, Michael almost lost all the confidence he had built up. What goes up must come down and his game began to suffer. The crunch came after another loss and, as legend has it, he decided to quit, but then Vincent van der Voort took him to one side, had a word with him and the rest is history. What knowledge was shared I can only guess, but it worked. Perhaps something like, 'I suggest you try it again, Michael, and let go of your conscious self and act on instinct. Stretch out with your feelings.' Which may sound like Obi-Wan Kenobi geeing up Luke (which it was) but said in a Dutch accent.

'If Devon won an event he would absolutely large it, if I won an event I absolutely give it ...' testified Joe Cullen. '[Michael] doesn't even flinch. He hits the winning double, it's very rare that he even gives a fist pump because it's that easy for him. He's got that much over everyone else. I don't know what it is, people lie and say – I'm confident doing this or that – but the bottom line is that if you play van Gerwen you have to play your 100 per cent best game and hope he doesn't.'

I began to doorstep Michael after his matches in the small tatty room that was set up for post-match interviews to keep the PDC internet and news animal fed with content. He would spot me a mile away and instantly look away. But I persevered. He kept winning, and I kept sitting there listening to the same set of general darts questions that are always trotted out. 'How did you play today?' etc, after being told not to ask any 'general darting questions' under pain of death. I toed the line and then after he won the 2017 World Championship I got to spend a bit of time in a room with him.

I calculated that MvG would have to win the world championships for the next fifteen years to equal Phil Taylor's achievement, and this is a good time to cut back to the conversation I had with him.

'So it's taken a couple of years to win this title?'

'I've been waiting for that for a few years and it took me quite long, to be fair, but it's been a phenomenal year for me. I worked for this really hard … I'm really glad it paid out … It's been absolute phenomenal for me …' Michael said.

'This season you've never actually looked in trouble …'

'I don't like to be in trouble, because when you're in trouble it's not really good. At the beginning of the final I was a little bit in trouble because I was missing my doubles and I could only blame myself for missing them, and after that I showed everyone what I can do with the 86 finish and I went into the break and after that I was there every set.'

'But how do you keep the momentum going?'

'You always need to keep believing in yourself even if you are 3–1 down, but the nice thing was that I wasn't 3–1 down, it was 2 all and I had the darts at the end, and yeah I hope I can do damage on that moment, as everyone was putting so much pressure on myself, everyone here probably, everyone at home, and probably myself even, more than everyone else in the world …'

'It must be weird to have all that pressure?'

'It's not weird it's just … I've found it really hard all year this pressure on my shoulders because I want to win it so much, it means the world to me and it also paid out and I'm glad.'

'How do you stay motivated?'

'It's not difficult as I love to win tournaments; that's what I live for. I had a phenomenal year winning all ranking tournaments and it cost me a lot of energy this year but I need to load up the batteries in the next month again. I go on holiday with my wife and afterwards I need to make sure that I'm ready for the Premier League again.'

'When are you going to slow down?'

'I will probably play as much as I can. I love to play darts and the best thing for a darts player is to try to win tournaments – what I like, what I love – and I like to play everything but sometimes it's a bit difficult because I have a family and friends and sometimes you also need to recharge your batteries.'

'Are you finally getting the recognition you deserve?'

'Yeah, of course it's nice to get recognition from a man like him [Dutch Prime Minister] and also the minister of sports, she went early on in the championships. But I still don't get nominated for sportsman of the year – it doesn't really matter as I showed everyone …'

'What did he say to you?'

'The Prime Minster said, "Could you believe ten years ago that you were going to win – for the second time in your life – the World Championships and also [attract] more than two million viewers in Holland?", and things like that. And that of course means a lot – recognition from a man like him – a powerful man, a huge man in Holland, the Prime Minister – it's a nice thing to have, isn't it, not a bad situation to be in.'

'Did you vote for him?'

'No. But still not a bad man!'

'Would you vote for him now?'

'No.'

'And how will you treat yourself?'

'I'm already treating myself in the last few years. I'm building a house, which is quite expensive so I need to make sure I keep winning otherwise I will need to stop building ...'

'What are the sacrifices you have to make to become World Champion?'

'The sacrifices are: anyone's family birthday I'm not there. During the Premiere League I'm only one day a week at home. I try to win this World Championship trophy and I'm glad it paid out now – that's the most important, it doesn't matter what sacrifices you've had to make because I've chosen to be a professional darts player and you always need to realise a lot of people dream to be a World Champion ...'

I felt chuffed, after having chased Michael about for an interview he never really wanted to give, I then spotted a news item on the PDC website, which showed MvG dressed in a Just Eat windcheater holding a Just Eat take-away bag, looking just like a delivery driver banging on your door after not being able to find your house despite his app and the GPS and now your food is cold and you're annoyed. Darts never fails to amuse.

'Mate, someone's got to step up to take him down.' Corey Cadby throws down the gauntlet. 'And I can assure you I'm the man to do it, when I take him down, he will be staying down.'

Interlude #8 – Kingpin

One moment I'm in the Empress room of the Blackpool Winter Gardens, which holds 2,000 and is one of the greatest darting venues because of the old-school architecture and abundance of chaos that is inevitably attracted to Blackpool; and the next I'm in the thick of it in the Etihad Arena in Belgium, which has a capacity of 21,000 and looks like an aircraft hangar, and as you join me it's full to the brim with European darts fans, who are pretty indistinguishable from the regular British ones I've become a bit more used to, who are all going apeshit, batshit crazy for the darts. It's total Babylon in other words, and so after a few minutes of madness I head backstage, where I randomly bump into Barry Hearn.

It's been a few months since we last sat down and I've travelled far and learnt much, and as I can't think of anything else to say I suggest we go and play a game of darts – and for a moment he looks at me like I'm mental, like I've not learnt enough, but then …

'Go on, then!' he laughs. The thing about Barry is that he will constantly surprise you, and add this to the fact that at every venue there is always a dartboard just sitting around, and that Barry likes to be totally hands-on, it's a good way for us to catch up.

At every venue there are rows of perfectly floodlit boards in the players' practice area, which are out of bounds for us mere mortals, but there is always a dimly lit board tucked away near to the media rooms as some of the backroom boys like to play and sometimes it comes in handy for the odd photo shoot. Barry and I locate the board, which tonight is tucked behind a huge gazebo that wouldn't look out of place in a garden party, but is used for the many on-line video interviews being produced around the PDC European Championship finals. I have a spare set of Phil Taylor cheap-as-chips entry-level brass darts which I flight up and hand to him. He weighs them up a little, as if to say 'how fucking heavy?' as I'm trying to get my South African flights into my Deta Hedmans but then we are all set.

I let Barry throw first just to gauge how good he is.

'If you had to give me one bit of advice, what would it be?' I open with.

Scoring Bed and Breakfast, Barry pulls his darts from the board and thinks for a beat. 'Life in sport is very similar to snakes and ladders,' he tells me. 'You spend your time training, working on your technical ability, dedication, concentration – all those sorts of things ...'

' ... are your ladders?' I'm a fast learner.

'Yes, but what you've got to avoid are those fucking snakes. And those snakes can be birds, drink, drugs, gambling, dodgy management, whatever. All that sort of stuff is very relevant as everybody is exceptional at one thing, because every human being is different. The sadness is most people never find out what that is. But it also follows that there is a level in all of us that we can go to. You could play darts twenty-four hours a day and never be as good as van Gerwen because you just don't have that something built into you somewhere.'

'That something is that I'm shit at darts,' I say, after throwing three darts that fail to either hit the scoring part of the board or stay in.

'But people like me – I have been an enthusiastic participant in virtually every sport you know, but unfortunately I've never been any fucking good. I can get reasonable through dedication. I'm a three-hour-twenty marathon runner because I trained. I knew that I was never going to be a two-hour-twenty runner, even if I trained eight days a week. It wasn't there,' Barry says, scoring a hefty 45. 'And sometimes you see these youngsters rocketing up the tables and yet they disappear as fast as they got there. They either reached their level or came across one of those bastard snakes.'

'And who should be looking out for those snakes?' I ask, throwing a very respectable 38, and things may be bad for the snakes and ladders, but they are looking up for my darts. 'Which players have caught your eye recently?'

'When you go through the top rankings now,' Barry says, 'do you want to look at someone who's ranked 100 and has got potential, or someone who is ranked in the top sixteen and could be in the top four?'

'I think the top hundred,' I answer. 'Always the outsider.'

'Then look at someone like Chris Dobey, who's mentored by Gary Anderson, and because of his results on the pro tour, which is the melting pot of how you get your ranking money, he has got a chance of getting into the world championships, where you get ten grand for turning up. Where they are coming from, that amount will pay for their year. And along the way they could earn some money as well ... Dobey has done enough in certain matches where I can see there is the potential there.'

'He's one of the teetotal ones!' I drop a bit of my new-found knowledge.

'Some of the names who have come up through the junior championship have never kicked-in and found traction on the pro tour,' Barry says. 'They may have found the devil drink, they may have just got complacent as all of a sudden they are earning forty or fifty grand and they stop thinking about how they can turn that into 400 or 500 grand.'

'And how would they make that next leap from making tens of thousands to making hundreds of thousands?' I really want to know, as by now it's obvious that we are both rubbish at actually throwing the darts; that our skills lie in other areas.

'You've always got to think poor in sport otherwise you just don't push yourself.' A pure corker of wisdom from Barry, which is more than I can say about where his arrows are falling.

'Anyone else you rate?'

'Outside of the top thirty-two, Joe Cullen, ex-postman, who's been on the circuit for five years. He's definitely one to watch.'

We play on in the half-light, with the crowds next door in the thick of it, going bananas whenever the darts song is played, which is pretty often *as each and every event revolves around the TV coverage. If it's not on TV then it's not happening.*

'What have you learnt about actually playing darts?' I have to ask.

'The most important thing in this game – apart from, yeah, of course you have to finish on a double,' Barry says in pure TV pundit style, 'is if you are a massive scorer you get more darts at the double; you get a bit of room to manoeuvre, and if you can finish as well then you are Michael van Gerwen.' And to prove his point Barry misses the board and almost bats an eyelid when the dart threatens to come straight back at him. Almost. He stands his ground, calm as anything, and not in the least bit worried that the dart may be on its way back to fuck up his expensive suit.

'I know I keep banging on about this, but why is it such a white game?' Here I go again.

'It's working-class white. There are lots of black and Asian kids out there who are still a generation away from playing.' Barry has a little think as he watches me throw my best darts yet and break a ton, and when his surprise has faded a little, he continues. 'Devon Petersen has got his own persona. He's a good-looking lad, and he comes on and does this breakdance thing when he comes in and he does this move with his hand … and turns the mirror on himself …'

'Who is your all-time favourite player?' I ask.

'You have to say Taylor has done an unbelievable amount. He can be annoying, but his record is just incomparable to any other sportsman in any other sport.'

'But, apart from winning, how does a player get to that level?'

'Everything is a soap opera in sport, and you need to get that mixture right. The secret of getting the soap opera right is that you don't change anything. You can't change a person as it comes across as fake. So you have to rely on what they are really like, but just maybe bring it out a bit more. So it's an art form, in a way.'

'And you first did that in snooker?'

'Yeah, we had the eight players. Steve Davis: White shirt. Drink water. You are the boring one. Jimmy White: Artful dodger. You can't read or write, but you can work out a six-horse accumulator faster than any man on earth. Dennis Taylor: Fat. Funny. Irishman. You tell jokes. Terry Griffiths: You're Welsh so therefore you think you can sing. So sing a lot and comb your hair all the time ...' Barry imparts a legendary slice of sports marketing history.

'Dope,' is all I can say as I throw my darts, but my enthusiasm is in our conversation. I know I'm privileged to be here with such a legend.

'And we literally went through the players like that. It was simplistic as it had never been done before. Darts is a bit more – let's help you with your walk-on music, and as they want the fame and fortune the players come to us with ideas.'

'And that works?' I ask in all honesty.

'People will buy a ticket just to watch the walk-ons.' Barry has a valid point. *'Five years ago you would not have heard of Peter Wright. He was just some bloke who played darts. He was okay, but then all of a sudden, give him a funny haircut and a weird suit, and get him to dance up and down ...'*

' ... and that made him globally famous!!!' I now understand.

'You go to Japan and 10 per cent of the crowd had a Peter Wright hairstyle,' Barry says, which brings me straight back to my moment at Wolverhampton eying up his wigs on the merch stand.

'It's the Grayson Perry effect. It wasn't his pots that got him famous it was dressing up as a little girl.' It's now my turn to offer a cultural insight.

'Correct,' says Barry, *'because it's all about perception ... and that is the common factor in everything we've talked about in darts. In a way, it's the greatest liability for the sport, and in other ways – if you take the*

perception on tickets, when you create that scarcity value perception, you've sold a show out.'

'Yeah. Like *Buzz Lightyear* or the *Nintendo Wii.'* Both marketing ploys I lived through thanks to my kids.

'The angle from us is through the creation of personalities and the deliverance of a value-for-money evening of entertainment, and so over a period of time – and we're not there yet – we are slowly changing the perception of darts and people are taking us seriously.' Barry has almost given up throwing. We look at each other and laugh. I'm glad he was as bad as me, would have been embarrassing for him otherwise. 'And they take us seriously based on real figures,' he continues. 'Ratings. ratings, ratings. And whilst we've got that we're safe, but darts fell out of fashion – late eighties, early nineties – and one of the reasons was that terrible [*Not The Nine O'Clock News*] sketch, which killed it. It was a funny piece and the public weren't ready for that perception. It wasn't that the ratings died, it was more that the powers that be took the holier-than-holy approach of "we can't afford to be associated with that, we'll kill it".'

'But it's not like other sports aren't just as dirty,' I add, dragging it down as usual.

'In today's world we can be associated with the Olympics with the drugs that are running all over the place. Sky can plough zillions into bike riding with half their fucking squad getting banned, all because somehow that perception hasn't filtered through.' This is Barry's last word on the subject. Magic Dave appears and signals that he is needed elsewhere. He hands his darts back, with that million-pound smile. 'Thanks, lad.' And he's off.

CHAPTER NINE

THE CALLER, AN MC AND A COUPLE OF WALK-ON GIRLS . . .

'"This game of darts is twisting like a rattlesnake with a hernia!" And to think that a snotty BBC bigwig once told me that darts would go on the Beeb "over my dead body".'

Sid Waddell, the godfather of commentators

THE VOICE OF DARTS

Sid Waddell was one of the founding fathers of darts, who until now – apart from the odd quote in this book – remained behind the scenes, a bit like reality. Sid was a Geordie, who grew up in the Ashington coalfield of Northumberland, in a tiny pit cottage in the village of Lynemouth – a hard, honest and physical place. He held a rare combination: the physique and health of an all-round sportsman with a bright academic mind. By eighteen Sid would split his time between A-level (or whatever they were called back in the day) revision and playing his favourite game of darts in the Black and Grey pub in Morpeth. He never really liked the competitive aspect of sport and when it came to darts he preferred to play games of doubles, whilst drinking cloudy, sweet scrumpy, throwing darts with the local farm boys. He captained the school rugby team, winning a place in international schoolboy trials, and was a finalist in the England Schools 100 yards in 1957, so sport was second nature to him.

'I reckon that my obsessive drive to get darts on to telly and later to commentate on the sport really started in that tatty Morpeth boozer all those years ago,' Sid recalled in his autobiography, *Bellies and Bullseyes*.

> I wanted to run like the great Jesse Owens. Darts was my own private theatre. I loved the bright spotlight above the board, the feel of the goose feathers on the bomber darts in the old George V Coronation mug besides the blind charity stocking. In a pairs darts match I relished the sarcastic banter when we put the whitewash on our opponents. I loved the meaty thunk of brass into flock. I loved the gut jolt when a double flew in. It was instant therapy for the grammar school's biggest swot, Bighead Sidney. I loved just the mere fun of chucking, boozing, chatting and not thinking.

Deep down Sid knew about hard work, and his relentless academic drive earnt him a full scholarship to St John's College, Cambridge University, and it was in these hallowed grounds of education that Sid learnt his first, and probably most important, darting lesson: never judge a player until you've seen them throw. They drowned their shame in booze after his college team took on some teetotal trainee vicars and got their asses whooped.

Fast forward (as we can do with the luxury of time) to April 1972 when we find Sid working as a documentary producer at Yorkshire TV in Leeds. He had just locked a film on Bobby and Jack Charlton, when he was called into the office of the director of programmes.

'Right, Boyo,' said a very Welsh Donald Baverstock. 'We want you to stop thinking about football for a bit and think about darts.'

At the mention of the word darts, Sid was propelled into another phase of his career. At this time, darts wasn't shown nationally or regularly on TV, and Sid was sent along to the *News of the World* Darts Championship final the following weekend to observe the production that went on silently behind the scenes and the cacophonic carnage out front. It was during this weekend that he first clapped eyes on Alan Evans, who lost in the final. The two men got to hang out afterwards and Alan was pretty drunk by this time, and was upset that he'd let his fellow Welshmen down by losing.

'I was convinced that lads like Alan Evans would soon be stars. Inside my working-class brain was this nagging revolutionary idea. Wouldn't it be great if darts got on to television alongside football, rugby, tennis and cricket? Inverted snobbery? Massive chip on Geordie shoulder? You bet ...' Sid went on the record saying.

A few days after his first visit to Ally Pally, Sid learnt that seven million people had watched the darts on *World of Sport*, which was one of their biggest audiences of the year. It was all the proof he needed that darts was a cultural and sporting movement that was coming over the hill of popularity.

The show that Sid produced was called *The Indoor League*, which was presented from 1972 to '78 by Fred Trueman – featuring a number of pub games such as shove ha'penny, table football, bar skittles, arm-wrestling, bar billiards, pool and darts – and shone a bright light on the unknown heroes who played them with some serious skill. (These are the 'Wheeltappers and Shunters' that Barry Hearn referred to.) The winner each week got £100, and the first series of the show only went out in the North of England. But after a tape was sent to the ITV bigwigs in London, and it was a massive hit in the north, a second series was commissioned for national broadcast. The show was aimed firmly at the working class and by 1975 was getting eight million viewers an episode, which, for something that went out on a Saturday lunchtime, was a huge number and proof that Sid and his team had indeed tapped into a sporting subculture. *Football Focus* would love those numbers!

Sid went on to make a great documentary about Alan Evans and the volatile, boozy subculture he was a superhero in, which he ended up making and broadcasting for the BBC, and entitled *The Prince of Dartness*. Once again, the film only went out locally in October 1976 and thanks to the feedback and the viewing figures, was broadcast nationally on BBC2 the following March. It's funny how the powers that be have always refused to see an (obvious) mainstream audience in darts because of their cultural blindness and have always to be proven wrong.

By the late seventies Sid was established as a serious current affairs writer and producer with many series under his belt, highlights including producing over 600 episodes of *Calendar* and working closely with Michael Parkinson for Granada Television. The working-class sports had slipped into the background professionally, but Sid was still loyally obsessed with pub culture the rest of the time. He loved nothing better than a drink or six, and a game of darts whilst shooting the breeze. A spot of boozy bants, indeed. In 1977 the sport department of BBC Manchester were setting up a team to cover the first-ever BDO World Darts Championship and as the producer had loved Sid's film on Alan Evans, he wanted him to audition as a commentator. You have to remember that even though Sid was a respected writer and producer, the thought of him commentating on the darts was something that he could only dream about.

'Commentator? World Championship? I was shaking like a novice whippet before its first handicap!' Sid swore off the booze, began to study the numbers – with darts it's all about the numbers – and went to the Club Fiesta in Sheffield to shoot a test tape commentating on the British Inter-County Knockout Cup final.

And with lines such as 'Those darts are thicker than Hamlet panatellas but they are caning that treble 19' and 'Jocky on the oche looking cocky', Sid spent the next forty years commentating and committing to tape the finest moments in darts, with a lyrical and vernacular style that he crafted and honed over the years, that was always true to his Geordie roots and his deep love of the game.

'The commentary on "sport in miniature", like darts and table football, which can be repetitive, must have vibrancy and attack in the patter. It is why the Dave Lanning style, littered with puns, became the benchmark.' Sid paid homage to his personal hero and groundbreaking commentator in his autobiography.

He wrote and produced many books and countless TV series and was also an immersive documentary film maker with his ITV series *Waddell's World*. From 1994 he was the voice of darts for Sky TV and was one of the many contributors that helped take darts from the smouldering ruins of the BDO train-wreck to the total global domination it's now about to pull off.

Sadly, after succumbing to bowel cancer, Sid died on 11 August 2012 and shortly afterwards the PDC renamed the World Championship trophy in his honour, which is no less than he deserved. Sid Waddell was a proper and bona fide gent who defined the true spirit of darts through his unquestionable love, enthusiasm and loyalty for the game.

THE FEARLESS MC

'I don't commentate. I'm just the announcer, the MC. I get the show going and then I introduce each player, as the walks-ons in the PDC is a major part of the show. They're characters who deserve a big build-up that I hope I give them.'

John McDonald

The first person I got talking to on this adventure was Dave Allen, the press officer for the PDC, and it was as I was chatting to him that he introduced me to a busy-busy John McDonald, the MC and host of all things darting for Sky TV. John was instantly interested in the book I was writing – and we struck up a fast friendship.

Barry Hearn may have granted me unparalleled and uninterrupted access to the inner workings of the PDC, but it was John who mined the actual coalface day-to-day and introduced me to the salt-of-the-earth people who make it all happen.

Most of you will know John: bright blue suit and white teeth with a big mic and a gobful of patter setting up each and every match on a screen near you. He who hypes the shit out of it, warms up the crowds (I've seen him work his magic on both the masses and the VIPs). After a serious accident as a paratrooper, John got on the media radar through his boxing and golf commentary, but it is for the darts that he is so well known. One fan recently came dressed as John McDonald, which must be an indication of how firmly John's star is set in the sky.

'I couldn't believe it. It was rather weird really,' John told me as we wandered about backstage, actually where all of our conversations took place.

Ironically darts was never of interest to John. When he was growing up his father was an alcoholic, and so John – naturally – had a real disdain for clubs and pubs.

'When I was a little boy I was brought up by my nan. Someone would knock on my door to tell me that my dad had fallen over and I would have to go out and pick him up. I hated alcohol when I was a kid. I was madly into sport but I think with darts you have to be introduced to it and the only way to do that is to go into a pub and I was anti that at the time. I never played darts nor did I know anyone that did.'

John's father has since passed away and after spending time in the military – where John learnt a healthy respect for alcohol – he no longer has a problem with people having a drink, which is just as well for all concerned.

In 2004 Barry Hearn – for whom John was covering the boxing – asked if he could host a pay-per-view darts event with Phil Taylor and Andy Fordham on Sky. 'I wasn't that interested as I didn't know that much about darts and I feel that you've got to know something about the sport to be involved in it.' John is one of those people who has a passion for everything he's done and wants to do it to the best of his ability, but he also spotted a gap in the market that wasn't being exploited. 'I was sure I could give them a better send-off and build-up. Barry wanted to do it like a boxing match or a big event – that's what he wanted to do with darts; he wanted it to be spectacular.'

It was a pay-per-view event that sold out. John grasped the opportunity with both hands; he thought long and hard about how he was going to introduce the players and did it pretty well, considering he didn't really know anything about the sport. But then disaster struck. 'I did okay, but about twenty minutes into the match I was looking at the monitor and there was no play. They just kept cutting back and forth to the studio and adverts and clips. I thought, Is the game going to carry on?' It was then John discovered that one of the players was unwell – he rushed backstage to find Andy Fordham seriously ill. In Fordham's own book he states that John helped him because he was married to a nurse, 'quite why he wrote that I don't know because I was a medic in my own right from my military training'. John certainly made sure that Andy was okay but the match was over Andy had actually suffered a minor stroke and had to have 18 litres of fluid drained from his lungs.

John drove home that night thinking that his introduction to darts was a complete wash-out; a shambles! 'I thought, God almighty – what have I let myself in for?' Even after Barry called him to say well done and that he'd done a good job, John wasn't sure that he really wanted to become involved in darts. 'Not thinking that there were many aspects of darts, I just knew what I had seen. And I didn't really like it that much. I thought it was a different business.' But Barry was insistent that that match wasn't typical of the sport and – more importantly – he had an idea for John to be involved from the outset with the team who would help develop the Premier League into what it is today.

This is when John started to study the game and as everyone he met connected to darts was so helpful, friendly, honest, his mind was made up. His opinion changed and he made the leap.

Eleven years later and John's still there, and some would say that he is better known for the darts than for any other sports that he's covered: the Ryder Cup, massive boxing matches at Wembley, blah de blah.

John has been involved in the PDC since 2005 and he was very keen to tell me that the professionalism he has witnessed is remarkable. After his initial reluctance he was bit annoyed with himself for thinking it would be otherwise. 'But you do hear these stories of people drinking and smoking, but now this is a serious business. Playing in front of packed audiences and that wouldn't be tolerated and I think that nothing like that is tolerated. The whole world has moved on and yes, of course there are players who don't like each other but that happens in every sport.' John is one of the sport's true ambassadors, not even my whiny pleading would get him to spill the beans on any major misbehaving, but it did lead me back to the subject of how darts is changing since leaving the pub.

'That is a very, very interesting subject because if you look at any decent sport with any longevity, they've always had to invest in the young. There is nowhere for them to go to become darts players apart from the pub. But now darts academies have sprung up and people go and play darts in colleges. You're going to see a whole new line of darts players because of the funds available – the winner's fee is right up there with any other top sport.'

One of the obvious developmental challenges is that the new generation of players will have played in a team or an academy to a pretty decent skill level, but will never have experienced what it's like to try to hit those doubles in front of a baying drunken crowd. One moment you're slaying some poor fucker in the Bridlington Bowls & Social Club, and the next you're wandering out onto the stage at the UK Open, in front of a few thousand people dressed as all sorts holding four-pint jugs aloft, going apeshit and singing about standing up if you love the darts, which is going to be a hard dose of culture shock for some people. For most. How you prepare yourself for that moment is the $64million question – or the $435,000 question if you manage to win the World's. And what about the dressing up? I thought John must have a view on this.

'The dressing up has become just part of the show. There is no demographic, as such, that defines a darts fan. You couldn't say it's 18 to 24-year-old men. It's not like that. You get old and young and families and children and fathers and sons. Every kind of demographic there is, you get at the darts. And the dressing up has become a major part. I don't know where they get so many costumes. Stormtroopers from *Star Wars*. The entire cast of *Only Fools and Horses*. Every superhero that's ever been created by Marvel. We've had the royal family and we've even had some real royal family. Judges and popes. Nuns and Jesus. Mexicans. Ten-pin bowlers.'

John took me from the back of the game right to the front. Literally. He was kind enough to let me shadow him as far as I could go, which was literally to the edge of the stage with everything across that line being beamed out live to millions via Sky. He gave me a really warm, honest and valuable insight into the world of the PDC – both back and front of house – and was always pleased to see me, which was extremely reassuring when I felt so out of my depth.

He is the popular, clean and scrubbed smiling face of darts and I know Barry loves him. He is everything that darts wants to be perceived as. Clean and sober and a bit cheeky but never rude or offensive – leave that to me. But will this be enough to push the game out into the mainstream and be forgiven for its smoky jokey hokey-cokey boozy past? Will the mainstream press ever really get off their lofty hypocritical perch and give darts the respect it deserves?

'You can't ignore the fact that darts has become a really popular sport to follow and during the Christmas period The *Times* and the *Guardian* and the *Observer* will do stuff, but I think it's their problem more than ours. Sometimes those newspapers set themselves on this big high hill – there is always going to be a tiered class system at every sporting event – from the VIP to the main floor. The majority of their readers come to our events so why wouldn't you report for them? It's their loss not ours.' And this loss is the slim margin where the brand hacks and the other assorted naysayers should be plying their trade to the millions of darts fans, most of whom have a disposable income (hence the costumes, the jugs of beer, the repeat attendances and the absolute fanaticism).

As we walk away a technician runs up and hands John something.

'What's that for?' I asked, ever the nosy writer.

'I've got an electric piano in my hotel room that I like to play at night and I didn't want to disturb everyone,' John tells me, pocketing the jack plug for his headphones before running off to entertain the VIP diners with his stand-up show.

WALK ON BY

From the moment I clapped eyes on that badly written sign ('Walk-on Girls' scrawled in green pen) on the 'dressing-room' door in Wolverhampton, I had to fight my gut instincts to question the backwardness and blatant sexism of the sole role of women in the PDC – the dolly birds of darts, to use a phrase from a time when men were men, etc. The shallow business-minded part of me that I use to try to understand what makes brands work won't shut up about how glamour plays an important role in the magic of the live TV show; how it's one of the elements borrowed from the WWF and an intrinsic part of what makes the PDC such a big deal. The writer in me wants to just shake the tree until the birds fly out of it and shout, 'This is 2017, for fucksake!' We no longer have to see Page 3 girls or read *Loaded* or *Nuts* or watch Miss World on TV, and yet here I am, sat in a Portakabin backstage somewhere, with Daniella Allfree (brunette) and Charlotte Wood (blonde). We're surrounded by hairspray and make-up and other such consumables, for I have entered the world of the walk-on girl.

Cycling and boxing also employ women in such a fashion – eye-candy, decoration, trimmings for TV. In cycling the debate to get rid of this ritual is more advanced, with the 2017 Vuelta a España including male 'podium assistants' and dispensing with the podium kiss for the winning stage rider. Perhaps this signifies cycling's full transition to the middle classes and a route that both darts and boxing will one day follow.

I was soon to discover (and so will you) that on the surface it's a bubbly bouncy glamorous snapshot of the most feminine side of darts. But what it turns into and what the subtext actually represents is a dark and dangerous tale of ever-lurking sexual violence; a world where your looks are omnipotent, and out of hours you are almost up for grabs. You are on your own.

The space where Daniella and Charlotte spend most of their time is far from glamorous. It's like a builders' canteen but with way more cosmetics and half as many electrical appliances. A small monitor sits in the corner tuned to Sky Sports Darts Channel, relaying what is going on out there in the front of house, a touch behind the action. A blip in time with the contrast turned up to 100. The crowd roars in reality and then a moment later on the big screens that flank the arena. Something happens in reality and after a touch of lag, it's seen by the wider world out in TV land.

'How do you define your job?' I asked.

'We walk the darts players on to the stage,' Daniella answered, without a hint of sarcasm or irony. She was just telling it like it is.

'Everyone thinks we hold a board up,' Charlotte added. 'Like in the boxing.'

'I've got a daughter,' Daniella explained. 'And I wouldn't feel happy doing the boxing, as opposed to this – this is such a nice job. So glamorous. We've been doing it for quite a while now, this is my fifth year. You become quite familiar with it as we do all the major events so the fans that do follow it see you a lot; you become a celebrity in the darts world.'

'What's going through your mind when you do a walk-on?' I wanted to know.

'When you first do it you feel so amazing. You look around and you get all the adrenalin, you really ride with it and you're absolutely buzzing to be part of it and as time goes on it just becomes ...' Daniella trailed off.

'Tonight, for example, it was fantastic to be walking down the ramp. It was ridiculous. But I suppose you do take it for granted a little, we're very grateful to be doing this job, we don't take it for granted at all, but when you're on that stage, when you actually really look – my God—' The thought of it made Charlotte go a bit quiet.

'It's wild out there and it's like really really brilliant, but when you're doing it at like Minehead, it's just walking and twelve or thirteen hours a day sitting in this trailer, it's a long day. Easiest job in the world, yes. It's hard being away and it's long hours,' Daniella told me.

And that is what the walk-on girls' job is all about: an instantly recognisable short cut to fame and glamour, but as seen and processed through the eyes of someone dressed in a shell suit, a Donald Trump mask, holding a handful of pitchers. There is no time for nuance or subtlety. I'm not going to say lowest common denominator, but then ...

'You do become part of the darts. People see you as such and we've done a calendar this year, which has just been ridiculous ...' Charlotte added some detail.

'We were asked to do that by the darts fans,' Daniella said. 'It was their idea. They said please bring out a calendar so we did it and it did amazing. It shocked me how many it sold.'

This is where I began to talk about back end and I mean the profit kind, not the grasping lairy lad sort, and they laughed and looked at me like I was a bit crazy and told me that it was their calendar, their piece of merch, and that they split the profits with the company who made it, who very kindly forked out the initial outlay (studio, photographer, printing, distribution) to get the glossy product to market. The *Daily Star* ran a two-page feature on it and the first print run sold out quickly.

I pointed out that for the first week of the World's there were some other walk-on girls, not the A-team, ones who I failed to recognise, the B-team perhaps?

'That's what William Hill call us. We're the A-team ...' Daniella told me, with a certain pride that the sponsors want to save the best till the last sixteen.

'We're both full-time models,' Charlotte added. 'And so we do other modelling as well. We've got families – to be here for the whole thing is a bit too much probably.' She thinks for a moment, before saying, 'When we're not here we'll get tweets every hour ...'

'But are you worried when you're not here? Are you always looking over your shoulder?' I had to ask.

'It is nice; it's lovely because you don't think they're gonna ... We always think they might like the new girls more,' Daniella added honestly.

'But they don't,' said Charlotte, stating their claim and asserting their rightful position as the hottest head girls of the school of darts.

But Daniella is still a little uneasy: 'We feel unsafe a little bit because of the job, because it's so desirable – the amount of people who message us after asking how we do it, how to get into it ... We've worked really hard ...'

And this is where I introduce the idea that perhaps the role of a walk-on girl should be more than just what they look like; should be more than just about the stunner on the red carpet.

'This isn't about what we look like, though. It's personality and everything else. This job is not just being a model and walking on that stage,' Charlotte schooled me.

'A walk-on girl's work is 90 per cent personality. We've had the most stunning girls doing this job and they've not quite got the presence on TV – you know, there is just something missing – you've got to have a little bit of charisma to do this, and I think that comes with age. We both started modelling when we were eighteen and we've both worked really hard,' Daniella said.

'We do love it,' Charlotte stated with such finality I had to believe her.

'It's short lived,' Daniella underlined the point with some cold harsh reality.

We'd touched upon something earlier that I had to return to. The potent combination of overt sexuality and social media – or to be more precise, those men who view women only through a lens of sexual gratification on social media streams.

'Do you get harassed for what you look like?'

'We've got a very big following on social media, and we've been so lucky cos we've literally had no abuse.' Daniella began to tell their side of the story.

'We don't get any hassle and if we do we don't see it,' Charlotte added.

'You get a few that are a bit sexual. Not terrible. Will you marry me, that kind of thing, which is a lot nicer than some things they've said,' Daniella confessed. 'But occasionally you will get some that are …' She trailed off.

'An arse shot that they've took from the side of the stage and then tweeted it out, which I think is very sly and creepy, and there are a few that we've had to block because they've been that much of a super fan, we've had full-on stalkers.' Charlotte began to chip away at the seal of truth.

'That's the main problem – the ones who become infatuated, like when they've sent us gifts and waited outside venues for us. We've had trouble with them, haven't we?' Daniella said.

'Yeah,' Charlotte replied, as matter-of-fact as can be.

Daniella continued: 'One sent my daughter presents – it becomes a bit scary because you do this job not knowing the impact on your other half …'

'They know where you live, they know everything about you. There was one the other week who turned up in a hat at the bar who had just turned up to see us,' Charlotte laid out.

Then I heard a story of a stalker (aka super fan) who travelled across the country and waited all day in the bar of an exhibition somewhere to see the girls for less than an hour. Charlotte's father witnessed it and couldn't believe that 'people exist like this that are so obsessed'.

I talk about having a beautiful 23-year-old daughter and knowing what it's like for a father who is concerned about how women are treated out there. It was at that point that I said that I was worried for them. Daniella had something to say to this:

'I couldn't sleep. The first year I did this was like my biggest, like, the craziest times with fans because I never had Twitter or anything and within a day I'd got thousands of followers. Crazy . . .' She paused for a moment to pull her thoughts together. 'I couldn't sleep for about a week and I got really, really upset. It would only take one person – a super fan – to come and say "do you know Daniella" to probably three people and they would find where I was, and at the time I lived on my own with my daughter. I thought we'd been thrown in here in the deep end. We've no security, don't know what to do . . . Mini-celebrities in the darts world and these crazy er . . .'

'But has the darts taken over your life?' I asked my final question.

'Darts has taken over . . .' Charlotte answered first.

'I'm worried about it a little bit because before we did this we were professional models, had a big client base, went to a lot of castings, and because this work has taken over I've hardly casted . . .'

'This takes over . . . there's no way it can't,' Charlotte underlined.

'The last walk-on girl did seven years . . . so for us to do another two years from now seems amazing,' Daniella perked up.

'We're not on contract, we don't know from one tournament to the next . . .' said Charlotte.

'The calendar was quite a test too, and it flew . . .' Daniella had the last word.

THE VOICE

'All right ...'

If there is one voice synonymous with darts, it's Russ 'The Voice' Bray. The clue is in the name, and every darts fan knows what he sounds like – a cockney growl that builds as he mutters the immortal words, 'Onneee huuunnndreeeed aaannnd eightyyyyyyyy.' The most downloaded darts app is the Russ Bray Voice Scorer, which is as train-spotterish as it seems. This is the future of darting merch. Just as the darting industry has to understand about the appetites of its younger consumers, it also has to see how darts sits in the digital space.

I met Russ at the start of this romp and at every event I made I said hello and paid my respects.

Russ splashes on the Brut, sports tats like a navvy, peppers his stories with liberal use of rhyming slang, and is as straight up a man as you will ever meet. I liked him immediately and he tolerated my queer ways admirably. His views and attitudes differed vastly from mine but friendship is about not having to agree with everyone all the time about everything, you get me blud?

Like most of the PDC, Russ started out as a player in local league and then county darts, where the matches followed the same format as the PDC today – i.e., you have officials and a caller. And one fateful night the caller for a game Russ was playing failed to rock up. 'I knew me numbers so I stepped in and helped call a couple of games and really enjoyed it and sounded all right. I'd played against the likes of Phil Taylor and Eric Bristow, but I was never as good as them.' Then, as fate would have it, the same caller (a slack fucker, by all accounts) failed to turn up for the next county game so Russ once again stepped up and called. His voice and style began to develop and he soon became the county caller for Hertfordshire around 1992–3.

And seeing he has such a dope-assed voice, I'm going to let him tell this bit of the story himself.

'Most sports people like one-on-one. One man verses another. You're not relying on someone else. If you're up there having a nightmare, you're having a nightmare and the only person who is going to sort that is you. That is why this game will always go forward. Always be on the top shelf. Because it's exciting because you get these boys and they put on a show, and it's a fine show and the skill factor of what they're bringing out is amazing. What one single man is doing with a piece of tungsten, that is why the game is so, so, popular.'

Russ's words lead us back to the classics, back to the gladiators, back to the basics of man vs. man. They also shed some light on why punters don't like to see women playing/challenging/beating men in the PDC, because it messes with their perceptions of what makes a proper battle. All macho bullshit, like, and that is why Russ's voice fits so perfectly with the overall image of darts.

'I'm not the best ref. I'm not the best counter. I'm the best known referee because of my voice. George Noble is the best referee, he's spot on. I'm not too bad. But I'm the one with the voice that is so different. It costs me nothing and earns me money.' Blinding – shit, he's got me at it . . .

To deconstruct it, his voice was born out of Essex but over the years it has been tempered into a Home Counties wide-as-fuck accent, and this is the perfect accompaniment to what is an all-round job of a caller: referee, mathematician, hypeman, bouncer. Russ has had to throw people off that stage as well as keep the players from twatting each other when it all gets a bit tetchy.

Our talk turns to how the perception of the game is slowly changing for the public, but not for the brand managers, and the fact that fewer players are relying on the drink to have a decent game. 'It goes back to the *Not the Nine O'Clock News* sketch. That hurt darts big time because it made people think that it was all about being a piss-head, but the modern day player isn't. It's not about getting on the piss and having a lot to drink and all the rest of it. The modern players don't have a drink when they practise, so why would they need a drink when they actually play? Jelle Klaasen doesn't drink. Ian White doesn't drink. Van Gerwen and Gary Anderson hardly drink. You've got all these boys up there and they don't need a drink. Darts has evolved from a pub game, which is what it was, but which it isn't any more.

'Look how far it's gone and how big the game is. It's the second most watched sport on Sky, and that's only after a big Premier League football match. It's a buzz.' And with this Russ strode off with his tom jangling and I couldn't help noticing a little swagger. If I was The Voice, I'd have a swagger too.

Interlude #9 – The road to Ally Pally

'Most pubs don't even have a dartboard any more. So you can't really call it a pub game any more …'

Russ 'The Voice' Bray

As you've read, I've delved deep into the world of championship darts, at almost every level. From the local right-leaning pub to the grassroots of the BDO backwaters of the youth system, from the next big names on the rise to actually hanging out with some bona fide legends of the game. So far almost everyone has been open, friendly and accessible; this is what darts is all about. The majority of the players are just like you and me, even though they are pulling in a million pounds a year or more. Most of the old-school players are like grizzly coach drivers with a bit more money but no additional airs, and a lot of the newer ones are just like the T.K. Maxx lads you'd meet in any boozer or club on the periphery of any town or city in Britain – your average lad gobbling down a Nando's or a Pizza Hut with a chaser of lager, wearing a Lyle & Scott jumper and some white Reebok Classics.

On 2 December I'd filled in the press form for the World's at Ally Pally, but as 15 December drew nearer I'd not heard anything back. I'd texted and called Magic Dave and each morning I scanned my emails like a kid opening his advent calendar, but to no avail. Nish. No fat choccy Rudolf or Keith or Bully. I called Barry Hearn and had a nice chat about the possible TV spin-offs to this book and how we needed to get together for a catch-up as things were shaping up nicely, all thanks to him and the access he'd kindly granted.

'I'm there all the time,' he said, referring to preparations at Ally Pally. And I arranged to meet him the next day at 5.

A few hours later my press accreditation came through and a massive weight was lifted. Ally Pally was the start, middle and end of this adventure and it had to happen. I am the biggest Tintin fan, but as unbelievable as it may seem I am way too old and overweight to even think about donning a sky-blue jumper and brown plus-fours, and a dollop of gel to make my quiff even bigger than it usually is. No. So my go-to fancy dress is the alcoholic, rumbustious, sweary Captain Haddock. Fucking perfect, my blistering blue barnacles. That and the fact that my wife and editor both thought going as a Mexican with huge cock-duster tash was just wrong. And possibly culturally insensitive.

Ally Pally is three stops from New Barnet on the commuter line. The train took eight mins but the walk up the hill took a little longer. For some reason I took what I assumed to be a short cut (we all know that assumption is the mother of all fuck-ups) and soon I was in a dark wet wood; the path turned to mud, but I could still see the huge radio and TV mast, which guided me through the mist.

Eventually my route converged on some steps and it was just at the summit of these that the glorious, majestic sight of Alexandra Palace rising out of the mist on a foggy London night halted me in my tracks. I'm hardly an architectural aficionado, but the sight of the iconic venue floodlit in the haze couldn't have been more impressive. This wasn't going to be some long-neglected provincial backwater knees-up. This was the World's. This was Ally Pally.

'It's incredibly different to the ones you've already seen!' Magic Dave had promised, as I once again claimed a spot in the warm and bright media room, but this time it was like a tsar's boudoir, complete with frescos on each wall, a couple of huge TV screens left and right tuned into the pop-up Sky darts channel and – more importantly – stacks of boxes of Family Choice biscuits in their glorious Christmas colours accompanied by a huge tea urn throbbing away.

I fix myself a cup of tea and look around at the assortment of international hacks and photographers sat at the long school desks waiting for the action to begin.

I set myself up with a space, plonk my Tintin bag down, and spread my notebook and pen about to mark my territory: I'm ready for my final term. I'm the only one in the whole media room who has bothered dressing up.

The fans' village is a massive hall chock full of food trucks and a big bar at one side. You can tell this is London, since the food brands on offer have more of a foodie vibe; a little less shit: Bodean's, Chicken Waffles, the German Sausage Company (I go for a bratwurst) and Hog Roast; there is even a cocktail bar, which is completely deserted.

Bald and short and wearing a warm coat, Darts DJ Lee spins the cheese high up above the William Hill stand, where if you can score over 101 with six darts they'd kindly let you wear a T-shirt advertising them all night. There is a massive queue and I stand and watch a few people miss the board completely and feel a little better about my own skills. Should have closed one eye! I think to myself. I am fascinated by the general public and their darts skills, each with a different style. Some great, some completely crap. By now I'm at a place where I know I'm rarely going to play without humiliating myself. I've almost given up.

I wander about costume-spotting (now part of my darts warm-up) and then watch a leprechaun and a Teletubby get some proper pat-down. It's a surreal and amusing sight to watch random popular children's TV characters getting frisked for contraband. I notice an 'amnesty bin' by the door and wander out to see what's in it, only to find it empty.

'Lucky man,' is the security guard's response when I flash my media pass to get back in.

'What's the amnesty bin for?' I ask him. 'Weapons and stuff?'

'Nah. It's not the football!' comes his reply. 'But I do the security for that as well. It's more for booze and food.'

'In case someone tries to sneak a picnic in?' I joke but he's not having it. The shine of my press pass has already run out and he tips his head as if to say, Run along, media boy, you're not clever, and I'm a bouncer.

There is a dartboard outside the media centre, just to the left of the TV tent (a small garden marquee sub divided inside into six small units from which to shoot video content, each with its own branded backdrop). Presumably for the players to do some publicity shots. I take out my darts and throw a few. I now know a bit more about the history and the characters who make darts so interesting and my enthusiasm had rubbed off on the people around me. My producer Dom had begun to send me videos – 'look what you've made me watch': Gary Anderson's nine-dart finish against Jelle Klaasen. My hairdresser (who we drive 200 miles up north for) genuinely loved the fact I was writing a book about darts and got all excited and nearly lopped off my beloved quiff. My mother (who I get my writing skills from) thought that I was in my element in the world of non-fiction.

The VIPs queueing up behind me begin to shout encouragement – You're shit! What time are you on? And by now my arm aches and, as this is technically bullying, I shake my head and scuttle back into the room with the tea and biscuits and TV and free Wi-Fi and young lads with radio mics and old men with huge lenses. One of them is the doppelgänger of Clive Dunn aka Grandad aka the bloke from Dad's Army with the small round glasses, and as he wanders past my desk he stops to talk about how there is only one person worth taking photos of – Gary Anderson.

'You've just missed me warming up,' I joke and he shakes his head and shuffles off.

I grab my iPad, walk into the main arena and literally bump into the Master of Ceremonies, John McDonald. It's then I realise that I've spilt sauerkraut and mustard down myself when scoffing the hot dog and a large lump of it has been laying in waiting on my access pass. Just after I hug John I look down to see the yellow peril and realise that a portion of it has indeed transferred to John's bright blue tie. He's on live TV in twenty-four mins (according to some techie) and my mind is racing as to what to do, as he takes me on a tour of his world, the unseen world of broadcast darts: from the hospitality suite where he will be singing a few numbers to the stage, then backstage, and the referees' stacked Portakabin. Which is where he leaves me to catch up with Russ Bray. When I mention Eric Bristow he just shakes his head as if to say, Don't even bother.

The main arena is full of long tables and stadium-style chairs surrounding all of this. On each table is a blue Santa hat and an oversized finger that says, I love darts. People are beginning to march in with their jugs and John McEnroe wigs and riding tiny polar bears whilst carrying boxes of wood-fired pizza stacked high and wobbly. These are the days of our lives. This is the night of all nights.

Each time I walk past a gang of lads I'm assaulted by a blast of aftershave.

The night begins: the dancers dance, the walk-on girls walk, the MC hypes the shit out of the place just as the TV cranks into life, the players wave and press the flesh and jog up the stairs onto the stage.

I spend the next fifteen days shuttling back and forth between my Barnet yard and Alexandra Palace and by the end can just about walk around unhindered, except when I try to go downstairs into the players' area. That is always out of bounds.

The William Hill World Championship continues a long-held tradition of darting competitions at Alexandra Palace and after being entrenched I can just about see why. It's a legendary London venue for a legendary English sport and it's also a licence for the PDC to print money. There was never a night where the majority of the crowd were not pouring down the cheap lager and consuming the above-average food, but all roads lead to the final, which is rapidly approaching.

CHAPTER TEN

THE EXHIBITIONIST

'Darts is one of the games that the general public can relate to, unlike being a Premiership footballer ...'

Joe Cullen

And just after the anthemic sing-a-long line of 'Chase the Sun' by Planet Funk drops once more, the lights go out ...

... the hall the size of an aircraft hangar goes pitch black ...

... and just for a moment ...

... all is quiet ...

... I'm stood in prime position to the right of the walk-on lane dressed as Captain Haddock. How the fuck did it come to this? I'm still cained from the New Year's Eve party a day or so ago as I hold on to the railings, waiting for the show to start, but one thing is for sure – I am ramped; properly excited. This is truly the climax – the 2017 final of the World's. Gary Anderson vs. MvG.

The lasers and smoke and incendiaries begin to do their thing and everyone is singing, chanting, roaring, as Gary Anderson does his walk-on with my mate Charlotte, who looks like she is having a good time and not thinking about the stalkers. Sounds like the crowd are certainly behind the Scot who looks like a Leith milkman or a National Express driver hitting the M1. He waves and kisses and slaps and does the old double thumbs-up sign as he makes his way towards the stage; a true re-enactment of the gladiator entrance. I'm way too busy shaking my fist – à la Haddock – for the photo opportunity to reach out and shake his hand. Then it's van Gerwen's time to shine, looking like a children's TV character, he mirrors the crowd's continued enthusiasm for eat, sleep, rave, repeat until he is up there on the stage and the battle can begin. Thunk.

There was never really a chance that the coach driver would beat the Teletubby. Never. Gary had a little glimmer of hope when Michael uncharacteristically missed a double 16 when they were a set and two legs apiece. But it was just a blip on the radar and Mighty Mike pulled his head in and his averages up and steamed off to win the title for the second time. That final dart was a bullseye, which I thought was a nice dramatic touch. A classic finish to a momentous journey, but it was also a nail in the coffin for my dreams of playing the winner, as MvG had made it clear he wasn't ever going to play a game of darts with me.

I was tolerated by the full-timers surrounding me in and out of the press rooms, often viewed as a curiosity and novelty, and perhaps someone they should keep their eye on. I pretty much behaved myself externally even when internally I was hurting somewhat. If I had pushed the boat out and behaved more like Hunter (which my gut was telling me to do all the time, would you believe?) the powers that be would have instantly revoked my press privileges, and this book would've been a feature article at best. Things done changed for your average gonzo writer.

I conducted over thirty interviews with as wide a variety of people connected to the darts as I could, looking for the most interesting, insightful and entertaining stories possible. I figured that if I was interested then you would be too. I started out with no knowledge and ended up meeting some truly magnificent characters. It's a pity that my darts games didn't improve but that wasn't because I didn't try. It was because I didn't have the motor skills and my dyspraxia got in the way, and talking of which …

PLAYING DARTS WITH TRINA GULLIVER

The week I started this book my old man had a hip replacement operation, which went swimmingly until a couple of weeks later he got on his bicycle (against my direct instructions – the old rebel), fell off and cracked open the almost-healed wound from the op. He didn't tell me about any of this and it was only when it had gone mouldy and started seeping that he said anything and he went back to the surgeon who had done the flawless op. He was shocked and sent my dad straight into surgery as the wound had become infected. He then spent five weeks in hospital getting a daily dose of industrial antibiotics to try to save his life. He's eighty-seven and fit as a fiddle but the infection could have finished him off. I was the one who had talked him into the op in the first place, and the thought of losing him totally freaked me out during this time and it was as I was coming out of Bath Royal Infirmary in the New Year – a few days after I'd come down from the final – that I got a text from Trina Gulliver, who was in deep preparation for the forthcoming BDO World Championships.

Trina was back in Cheddar and I was only half an hour away. My brain was racing. After MvG became World Champion I knew that there was no chance of me playing him, so I needed something a bit deeper to go out on. My double top, as it were. Then I had a brainwave.

'You want me to come and practise with you?' I texted back. There was a bit of a pause.

'Why not!'

'I must warn you that I'm dyspraxic and my darts don't always go where I want them to.'

'Do I need a hard hat?' she joked.

I wheeled my old man back to his bed and gave him his books and clean pants and the next thing I knew, I was driving through the dark countryside. The drive from Bath to Cheddar was even more long and windy as this time I was properly shitting it. I was really upset about what my dad was going through, and I'm no good at darts and I'm off to play one of the greatest ever champions … it all added up to a bit of a head-fuck.

I walked into the pub and found Trina warming up in the sports bar side.

I fumbled my darts out of their case and struggled to put the flights in. I put this down to nervousness but in reality it was because I'm just a klutz. I managed to get two in okay but the third was somewhat elusive.

'Do you want me to do that?' Trina offered kindly.

'I've got it,' I braved it out, hoping that things would get better, and eventually got sorted.

'Right, let's warm up …' Trina showed me how to stretch and warm up your arm before you play a game. I stood next to her on the oche and we stretched together.

'Where do you normally practise?' I asked.

'Right here.' Meaning the oche of the Riverside Inn, Cheddar.

'When you practise does someone play with you?'

'I tend to play on my own. My own routine.'

'Is there any way of upping your game?'

'I give lessons …' she said, and I really began to fumble with the darts. 'It all depends on what attention to their game needs doing …'

'I think I got it.' Pride always comes before a fall, or so I'm told.

'Stretch your arm off first. When I give lessons. I always tell them to stretch off. It's a sport, you're using your muscles.'

'Did you ever play Bristow?'

'I worked with Eric doing exhibitions … He had the attitude and got away with it. You either loved or hated him …'

'So I heard!'

'So you don't like any sport whatsoever?' It was Trina's turn to ask a question.

'No,' I answered. 'I like reading and writing books. And that's it. I only did this to learn and document the journey.'

'I don't like practising at home as I find it boring. How much time depends on what tournament I've got coming up and how much practice I feel I need. If I'm not enjoying it, I just walk away cos all that does is put negatives in your head. If you're playing really well then you want to play for longer anyway …'

And to demonstrate this we then played a game of 501 for real and it was over really quickly. What did you expect? There I was, stood at the oche with the greatest (in all senses) women's player of all time and I was trying my hardest to hit the treble 20 – and yes, before you ask, I had one eye closed – it was a whitewash. I got to about 400 and Trina checks out on a double 16.

But the point is I came, I played, I lived that moment. Trina was a good sport.

THE REAL CIRCUS CIRCUS

I'm driving around the M25 when it turns into a car park. It shouldn't've been much of a surprise as it was a Friday afternoon and I'm approaching the Dartford Crossing, but all I can do is amuse myself by thinking about the evening ahead; dreaming of what may go down:

I pull into the tattered car park of the Circus Tavern, for the Masters of Darts night with a host of darting stars, both past and present, grab my darts off the seat and walk in. To the left of the door as you enter, set out on trestle tables like a comic convention, there is a stand selling all manner of darting equipment and the like. The venue smells like it looks from the outside – slightly rank – but it's abuzz with a certain type of punter, the older more mature darts fans, and a guttural chatter fills the air. This place is a strip club by day, after all.

I walk up the dark staircase to the top bar, where the VIP meet-and-greet is being held, and I'm greeted by a friendly lady in what looks like a modified business suit, oversized glasses and a pair of polished enhancements sticking out like the ledge that John McClane held onto in *Die Hard*. This may be a darts night but there is a lot of heavy cleavage on show. Through the mist of my dream I can first hear, then see, The Voice, holding court at the bar in a black suit, black shirt, and a pink tie and I go and pay my respects, and by the time he recognises me I feel like a right tit standing there smiling like a goon, and back straight into the larger-than-life figure of Bobby George who is drinking lager and chatting to the evening's host, Keith Talent.

'Did you invite Martin down?' I ask Keith but this draws a blank, and I turn back to the bar and order a pint of shandy. The bar – to gauge the theme, think of a Chinese restaurant in Warrington or Hemel Hempstead and then let it age a while – is full of people who are either guests of the players or have stumped up £40 to be able to spend an hour up here meeting-and-a-greeting before the darts begins downstairs in the main part of the Circus Tavern.

There is a dartboard down a couple of steps, and as I wander down, I realise that the very first person I ever saw playing darts back in time in Wolverhampton is warming up with a few crafty arrows. I down my pint and pull out my own set – which I've already flighted (if that's the correct term), ready for action.

'All right, Phil,' I say, as I mooch over. 'It's Adam from—'

'Wolverhampton press room,' Phil finishes. 'I have a brain, you know.'

'Do you mind if you give me a quick game?' I ask, absolutely shitting myself.

'Sure. I need to warm-up against someone decent,' he quips.

Phil throws 140 and I don't get anywhere near a quarter of that, but all the darts hit the board and no one is hurt. We play on and people are watching and it's clear that one of us has the skills to become World Champion sixteen times and the other doesn't.

I score 66 and then I remember about shutting one eye, which I do and almost fall over. Phil hits a 180, pulls out his arrows and then gives me a look to say, Get a fucking move on, and I walk up and throw my darts.

I score a little better than before but nothing to write home about.

Phil throws quickly and scores 120. As he is retrieving his darts he turns and tells me: 'If you can beat that then I'll concede.'

I walk back over, close one eye and throw for my life.

The first dart lands in the 20. The next in the treble 18. The last in treble 20. This is the highest I've ever scored in my life.

'One hundred and thirty-four!' booms The Voice, who has quietly slipped over to watch the action unfold. And this is the moment that I realise that it's never going to get any better. I've just beaten the greatest ever darts player in a game of darts. And that was the end of my darting adventure.

And then the bloke in the car behind me gets the hump and really lays into his horn.

'Okay!' I shout, snapping back into the traffic and the haze of the damp February evening in the glorious confines of the M25. I was properly enjoying that!

I park in the car park that has a thin layer of cracked and filled tarmac spread over it like Vegemite on toast, of the Circus Tavern, venue for the Masters of Darts night featuring a decent amount of past champions, one superstar, and the up-and-coming Jelle 'The Cobra' Klaasen. There are a few people sat in their parked cars who all watch me like a hawk as I get out with my darts. It feels a bit like a dogging hotspot and I hurry inside to escape the cold and whatever else. I go up the stairs to the VIP – as directed by the woman in the box office. As I step into the room I am struck by a surreal scene: a busty barmaid dressed like a businesswoman is pulling Bobby George a pint, Wayne Mardle is telling a joke, and Keith Deller is telling the voluptuous lady behind the bar to charge everyone for drinks, even the soft ones.

I wander over and let Wayne land his punchline and re-introduce myself to the man Martin Amis based Keith Talent on, and this is when the wheels fall off.

'No,' he says, shaking his hair gel. 'I told you the other day you can't come down tonight.'

'But ...'

'Sorry, it's a busy night and if you want to buy a regular ticket I can't stop you, but you can't come up here,' he tells me. 'This is for VIPs ...'

'And there are no VIP tickets left! Otherwise I would have bought one.'

'No can do.' He isn't budging and this isn't about the numbers on the night.

'I just wanted to—'

'You have to leave ...' Something has annoyed this man – perhaps there is a clue buried somewhere deep in the narrative but I sure as fuck don't know what it is. The place is empty. It may well fill up but it's hardly some state-of-the-art night spot. One more person (who is already there) is not going to make any difference. This is clearly about me. I turn and leave as quickly as I entered.

Driving home on the M25 my phone goes and it's a Brentwood number, location of the PDC headquarters. I answer it hoping that I'm getting called back as this has all been a bit of a mix-up, but it's not, and I'm in trouble. Worse than that it appears that I'm out of the inner circle of darts. Keith Talent has got straight on the phone and called Phil Taylor (who I was supposed to be meeting at the Circus Tavern) who then got annoyed and called Magic Dave who is now calling me to give me a right bollocking.

'I only went in to say hello to Phil and to make sure he remembered me from Wolverhampton.' I presented my case.

'I can assure you he doesn't,' says the voice that was once warm and friendly but is now stone cold.

'There you go! That's what I'm saying. That's why I dropped in.' I made my case.

'And now Phil's annoyed that he was called about your hanging around, and he isn't going to give you that interview.'

'Really?' And at this point I am gutted as I realise that I've inadvertently fucked it all up. 'Sorry – I was only being keen. Wanted to put a face to a name and hopefully get a game of darts with him.'

There is a massive pause on the phone. Like fucking huge. 'That was never going to happen,' came the delayed reply as deadpan as can be.

'I realise that now,' I say, all crestfallen. 'Do you think there is any chance of a phoner?'

'I'll speak to Barry on Monday, but I can't promise anything. Not after today.'

The call ends. I crawl along the M25, take a deep breath and pull myself together.

Interlude #10 – The end of fear

> 'The decline of the trade unions lies at the heart of many of the problems
> of the working class: the fact that they don't have a voice; their stagnating
> wages; their lack of rights in the workplace, and so on. The demonisation
> of the working class is the ridiculing of the conquered by the conqueror.
> Over the last thirty years, the power of working-class people has been
> driven out of the workplace, the media, the political establishment, and
> from society as a whole.'
>
> Owen Jones, from his book Chavs

In the above statement you could easily replace the words 'working class'
with the word 'darts' to highlight one of the recurring themes and areas of
interest for me, on my gonzo journey through the world of championship
darts. Darts stands out and stands proud because it is raw. Be that
smoking, drinking, gambling, taking drugs, on or off the oche. The power
from this unalloyed authenticity is what has driven the sport forwards
since the first News of the World Championship in 1927, and what
initially caught the eye, heart and mind of first Olly Croft and then Barry
Hearn, two very different godfathers of the game.

At first I thought that this book would be about immersing myself into
an arc of subculture that I'd previously neglected – the white working
class, which in some ways it is – but more importantly this is a book about
the culture of losing. No, really it is, and there is nothing wrong with the
queer art of failure, as you have to go through it many times in order to
succeed. Every legend has lost at one point in time. Look back to the most
powerful force in darts today – Michael van Gerwen – who had such an
unsuccessful period when he made the transition from BDO to the PDC,
so much so that he nearly slid his tungsten back into the lime green pouch
for ever. Think for a moment about if he hadn't had the chat with Vincent

van der Voort that subsequently propelled him on his way to becoming the second greatest darts player of all time, Michael would be fixing some poor sod's roof in the Low Countries dreaming of how he could have been a contender.

And when you look at the art of losing from the other angle – where in sport can a complete rookie end up playing a game against a world-class master? Once the player gets his first PDC tour card – his 'Willy Wonka golden ticket' to quote Barry – that means he can be drawn to play The Power, Mighty Mike, The Flying Scotsman, or the Cobra in the next competition whilst still being completely wet behind the ears. Like a fucking lamb to the slaughter. Think back to the rosy-cheeked Max Hopp having to walk on stage in Wolverhampton to face the full force of van Gerwen, who can play like no one else right now – although sat here typing this, Devon Petersen has just informed me via a Twitter message that there is a possibility of a chink in the armour, a crack in the Achilles heel of MvG.

'He is showing signs of being beatable, as this weekend he lost in the final (of the Happy Bet German Darts Championship) to Peter Wright. It may be the turning of the tide and has made us all excited again …' and if Devon is about so is his broe:

'A lot of it is confidence. Michael is a good example even if he is head and shoulders above everyone at the minute,' Joe Cullen weighs in. 'There was a little spell in the middle of the year in the World Series where he got beat by Anderson and by Phil, and he showed that little bit of vulnerability – but it's the confidence. If you're stood behind him you're always thinking that you've gotta hit the double, whereas anyone apart from van Gerwen, you think – I might get a little sniff at this – but if van Gerwen is at it you know you're not getting a go. But that's his power as you've already succumbed to the reality that you're not getting a shot, and when you do you're surprised and then he might still snatch it. He's an animal at the minute …'

And for darts to reach the biggest audience yet, it needs to lose the rawness, which was what made it great in the first place. Catch 22 and then some, all the while live on a Sky TV feed.

'Everything Barry does is focused around TV,' said Leon Davis, a very educated black man in a very raw white world. 'He looks at the markets where they have big TV share and puts on an event there. It's all to do with TV. And that way it's similar to football, TV is central to a sport being popular, that's how it globalises. That's the medium that makes it the attractive product that it is, and the way the PDC works with Sky and other broadcasters is what makes it so successful today . . .'

Darts won't ever really disappear back into the subculture like it did in the mid eighties, because the masses won't turn off from it in the same way as they did the first time around. In cultural terms the main event surrounding the sport has become what's popularly known on the internet as a 'thing': an organised activity like paint-balling or go-carting but with way more booze and a little more carnage. In the eighties darts was always looked down on as a bit of a working-class novelty, a pub-based pastime that Guardian readers would dip in and out of when they fancied slumming it. The Not the Nine O'Clock News sketch was the cultural, and yet beastly, nail in the coffin, but this time around darts occupies a different space, and one that is not as easily rattled. The media and its associated literati operates under a different set of rules and a couple of Oxbridge-educated comedians (as they were back then) mercilessly taking the piss out of a slice of working-class culture (that they knew nothing about) today would not make the slightest bit of difference to how people choose to spend their free time and hard-earnt cash. The sketch exploited a weakness in the minds of the chattering classes about something that they didn't really get, that they were never an integral part of, and it was a slice of popular – disposable – culture that was already being tampered with on a day-to-day basis by those who made their living 'writing' for the tabloid press.

In business terms, darts has become a major industry employing thousands and catering to millions, and generating hundreds of millions of pounds – and this means it will be sustained by any means necessary. Sat here writing this, it is safe to say that darts is about to reach another critical mass right now in terms of scale and audience size and profitability, and once this is achieved it won't last for ever. The big wheel keeps on turning, day-by-day, and these will be the glorious golden salad days as everything has a finite life span. Once the public's appetite begins to shrink, the PDC will have to examine and dissect the habits and behaviour of the audience that brought it to its peak and sold out the big arenas. The main change was the venues of the big shows – that were previously held in exhibition centres and civic halls – they have now moved to the biggest arenas in the country. If a drop in attendance occurred, they might have to downsize slightly, but the other way that they could sustain the momentum would be to focus on Europe and other emerging markets such an Australasia and the Commonwealth regions. They would need to globalise in order to shift more product (tickets, beer, pizza, burgers, multicoloured Mohican wigs), and this would mean some kind of compromise with the USP of darts. This would mean a more extreme commoditisation and mass-marketing the game. The fact that Rotterdam sold out in nine minutes is enough for the PDC to know that it's time to expand their operation into other places, such as Holland and Germany. The vibe will be different in these territories anyway, because it hasn't come out of the pub.

But never mind that, here is some food for thought, from one of the definitive long-form pieces of journalism written about darts by heavy-hitting Aussie sporting academic Steve Georgakis:

Professional darts is largely played by overweight, middle-aged white guys who drink lots of alcohol and have lots of tattoos. While they are only allowed to drink water on stage, it is not clear if many of them could run 100 metres. There is a paradox. The sport's rise at the elite, commercialised level has: coincided with a decline in participation; resulted in prioritising entertainment over sport; associated the sport with negative social forces; and promoted the players, who are hardly positive role models. So the hard physical outcome of the above is the inundation of really questionable sponsorship.

The future of darts lies in a dichotomy: on one hand the powers that be have to allow the sport to breathe and grow and shed its working-class image in order to attain the perception of a world-class sport; but at the same time they must ensure that it keeps its integrity and soul, which as we've seen emanates from the grit and the dirt and the pure realness that is ingrained from its place of genesis: the boozer, which is rapidly becoming a thing of the past.

It's a bit of a fucker. If it goes too far either way the trajectory of the sport will stall and it may never reach its full potential. It's all about finding a balance, and maintaining its perceived value with Sky, as one thing is for sure: sport is only as powerful as its visibility, and that falls back to getting on as many screens as possible.

No one really knows what is going to happen in the future and whether darts will remain relevant, but one thing for sure is that as long as Barry Hearn is the chairman of the board, darts is in the best possible hands ...

ACKNOWLEDGEMENTS

Lots of peace + love to the following who helped me on my quest:

Trina Gulliver, Barry Hearn, Irvin Welsh, Russ 'The Voice' Bray, John McDonald, Devon Peterson, Corey Cadby, Joe Cullen, Max Hopp, 'Magic' Dave Allen, Jake Hanrahan, Steve Cording at The Evening Standard, Leon Davis, Bob Potter the legend of Lakeside, Olly Croft, Martin Amis and Keith Talent, Danielle Allfree and Charlotte Wood, Phil Taylor, Michael van Gerwen, Matthew Porter, Deta Hedman, Martin 'Wolfie' Adams, Sue and Wayne Williams, a grateful nod of thanks must go to Keith Deller for playing the panto baddie to my cinderella, Arlen Figgis for shooting the film, and last but not least a double helping of thanks for Tim Broughton for having the brilliant idea of asking me to write this book, even though I know nothing about sport of any kind whatsoever (and still don't).

A big family 'Yo Peeps!' to: Wilma, Kaiya, Casius, Rhianna, Jessy, Andy, Dave, Jono, Jayne, Francesca, Lizzy, Delphine, Lizane, Chris, Toby, Naughty Betty, Mickey, Lindsay, Elodie, Dom, Thandi, Alex, down under Jimmy Dodd, Pilpeled.

The special award for divine inspiration goes to my little sister Tara for listening to me on the phone that time when I was waffling on about finding a narrative for this here book. Thanks sport.